DEEP IN THE JUNGLE HE
LOOKED FOR GOLD, ONE DAY IN
THE EARLY MORNING HE FOUND
A GIRL SQUATTING IN THE GRASS.
HE WATCHED HER. SHE SMELLED
HIS BODY. "WHAT?!! SHE SAID,
>> OH HI
>> ARE YOU WATCHING ME URINATE?
>> YES,
>> WELL PLEASE STOP.
>> OK.
HE CONTINUED ONWARD, HE WAS
FEELING PERVERTED, BUT
IT WENT AWAY EVENTUALLY. A
TALKING MONKEY SCREAMED AT
HIM.
>> AAAAAAAAAAAAAAAAAAAAAH

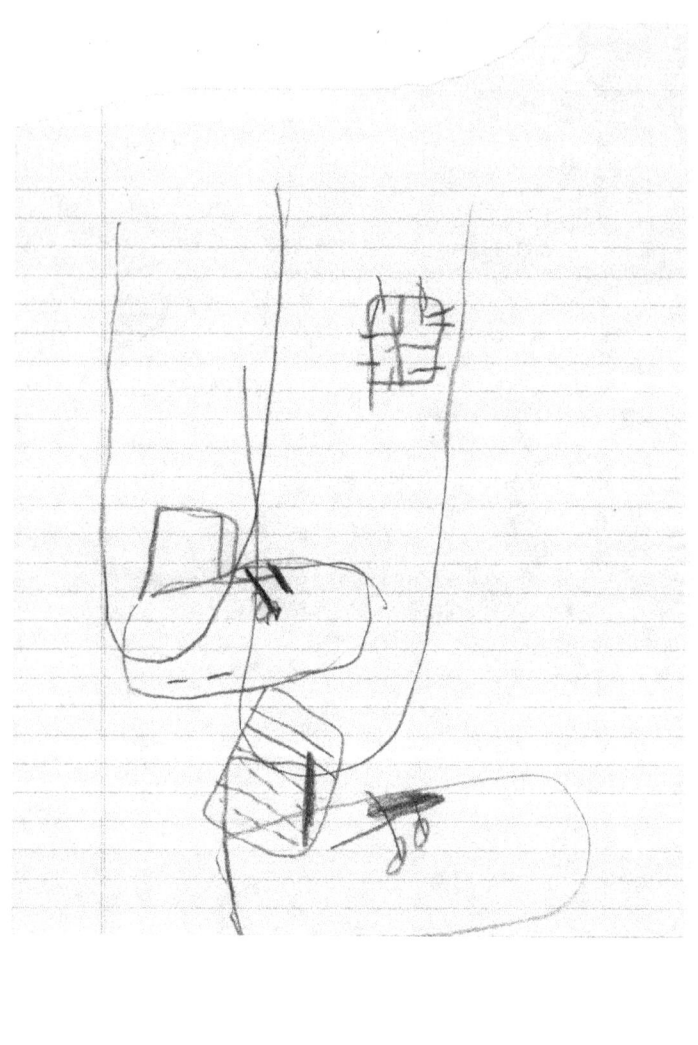

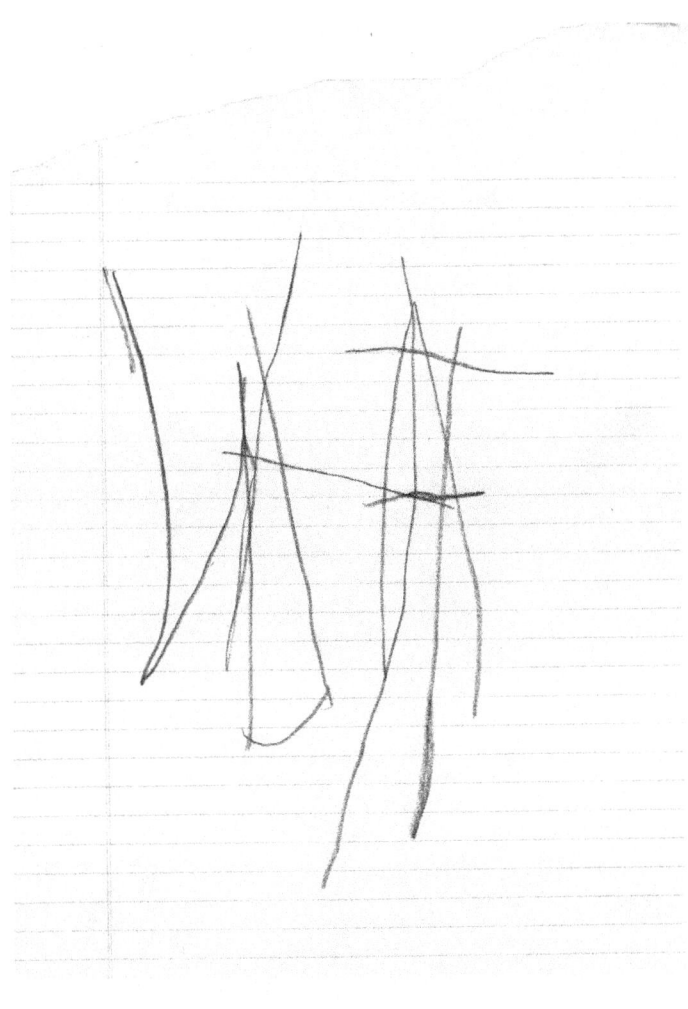

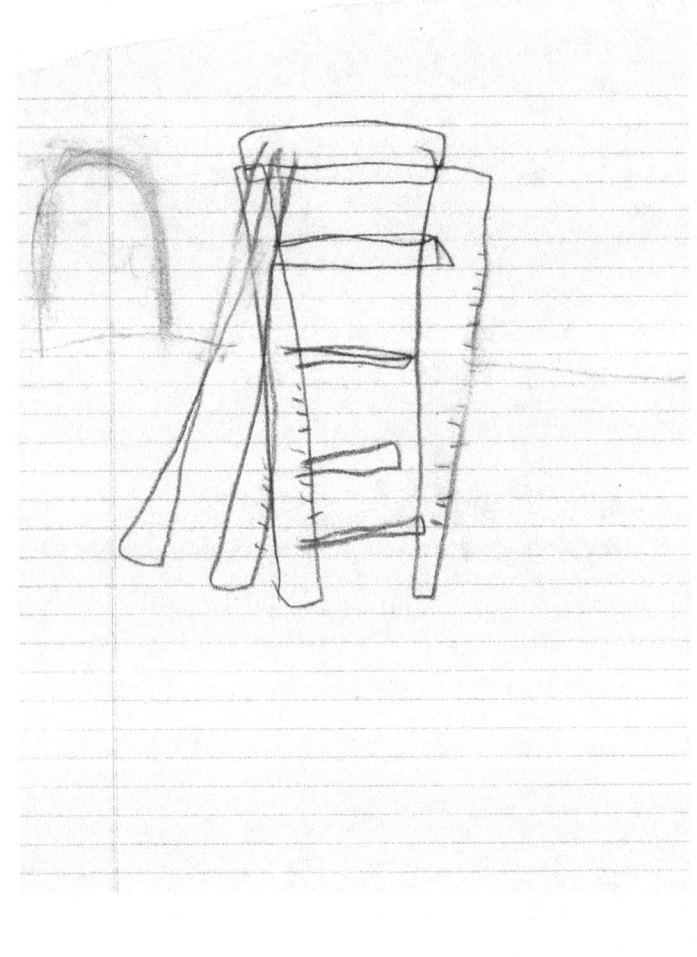

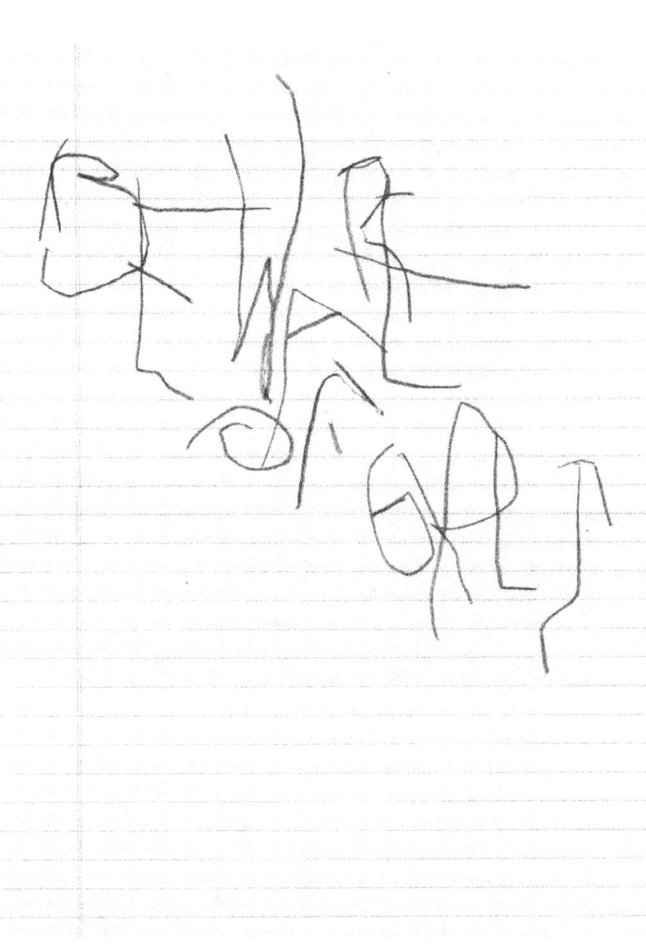

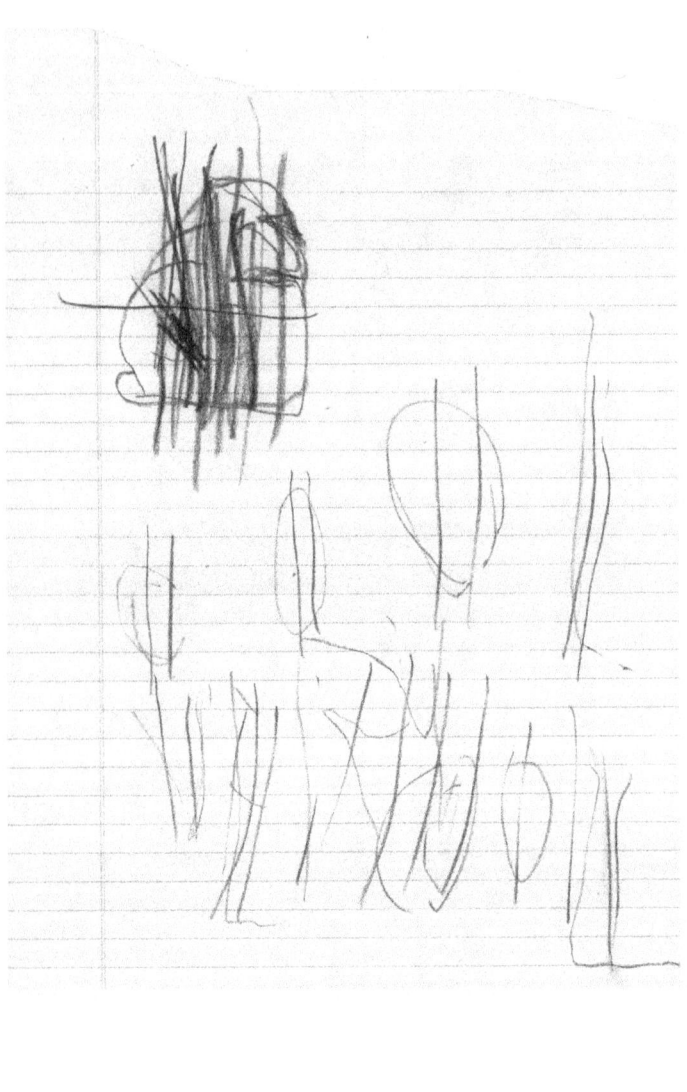

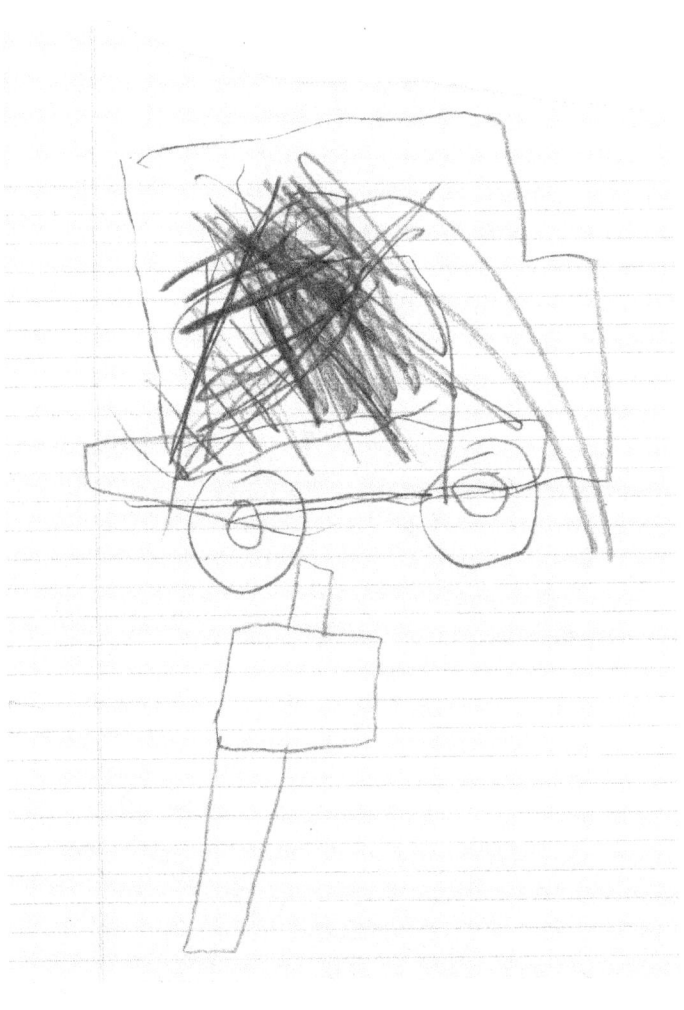

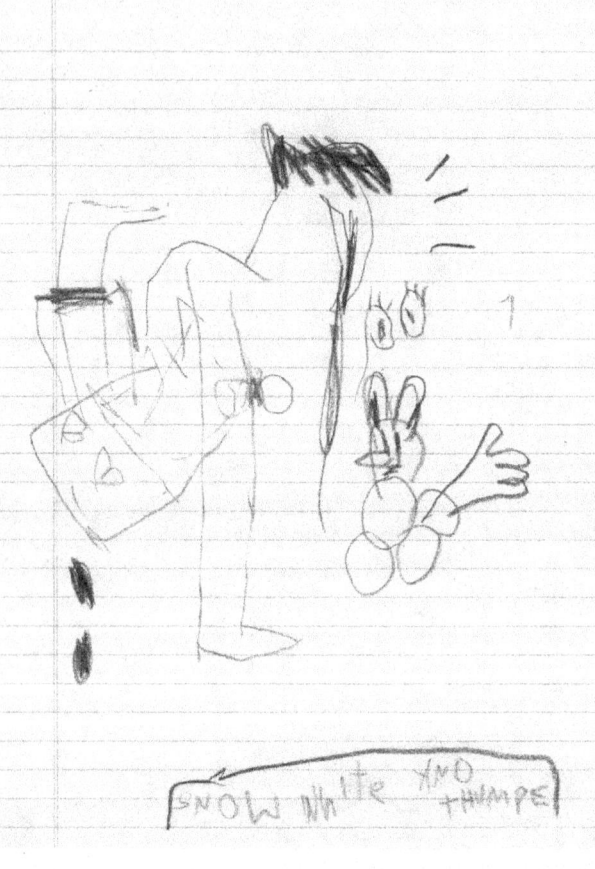

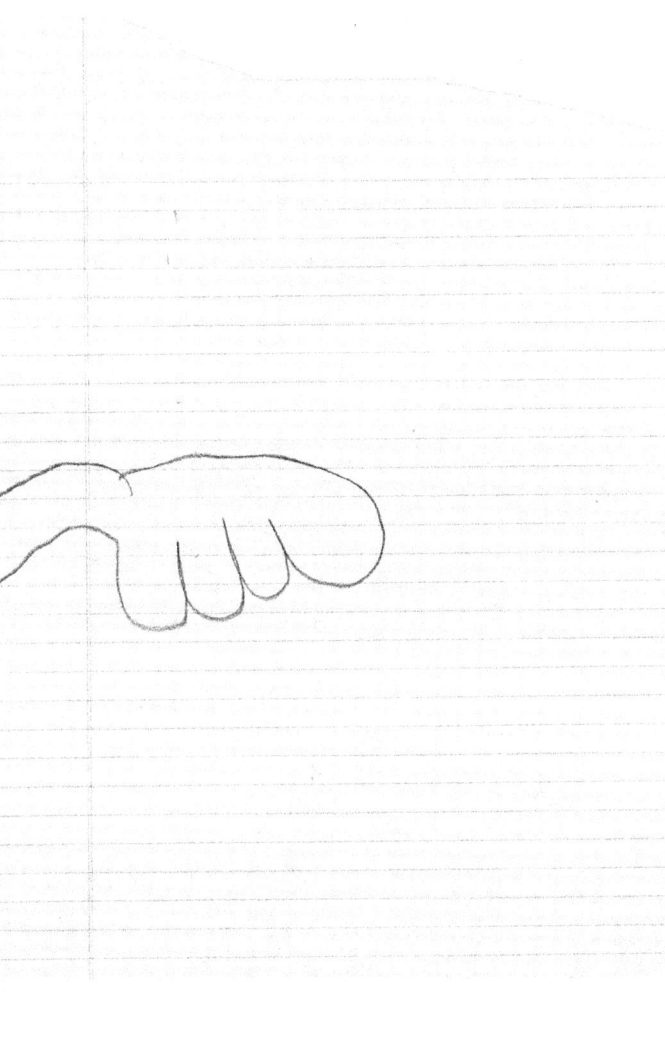

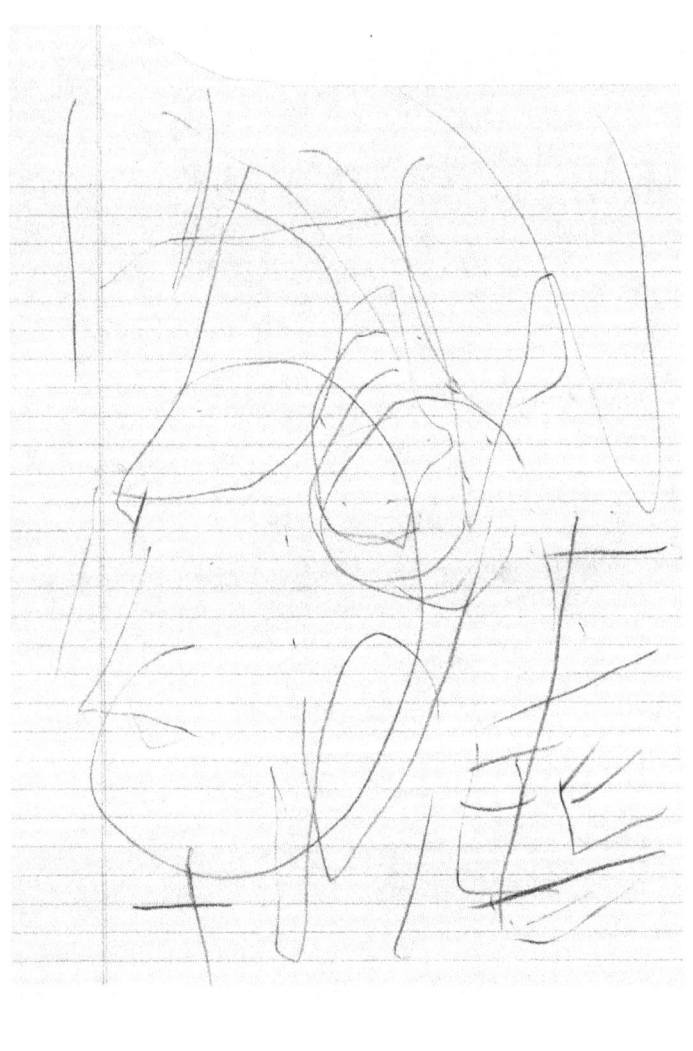

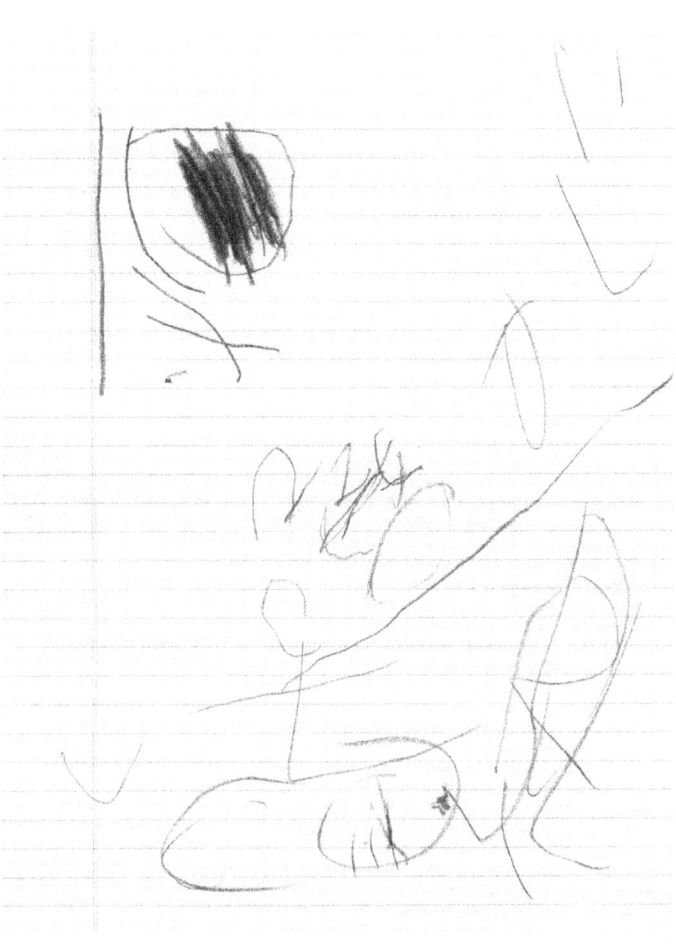

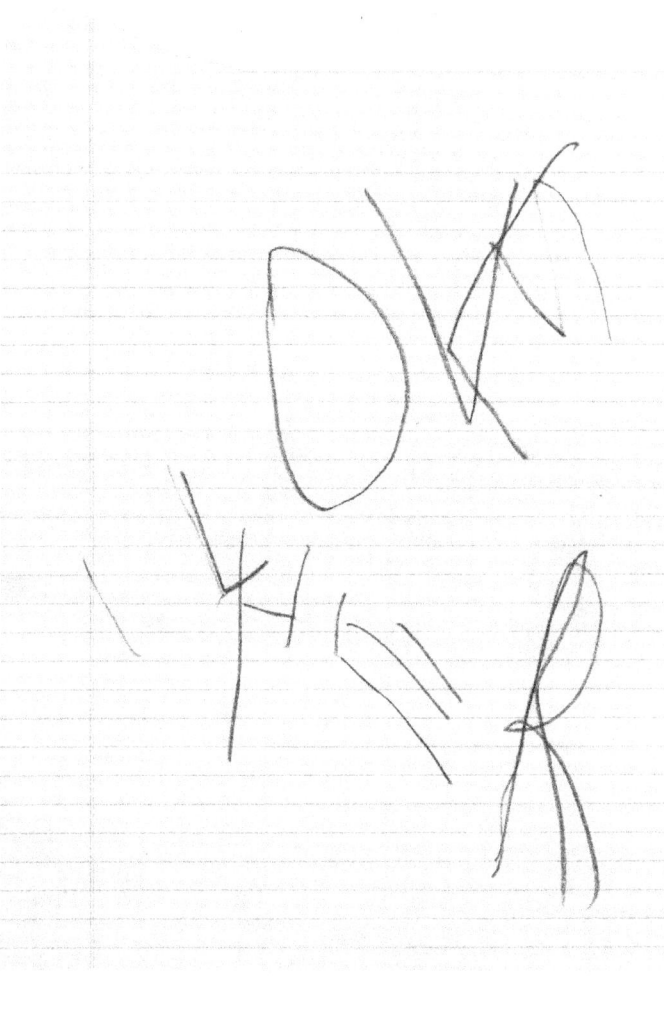

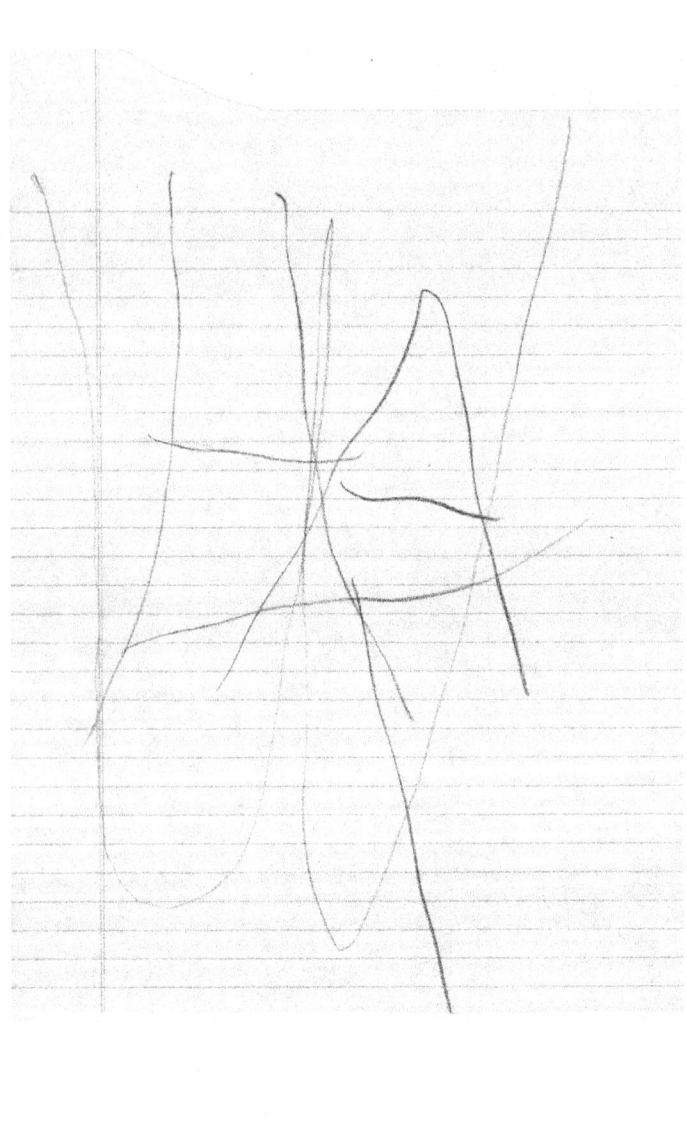

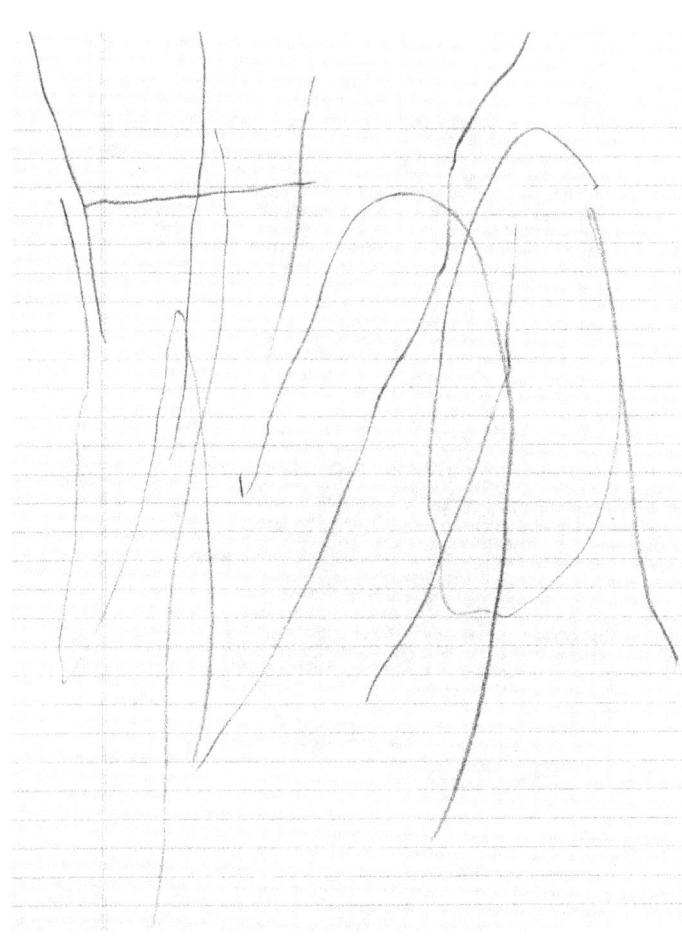

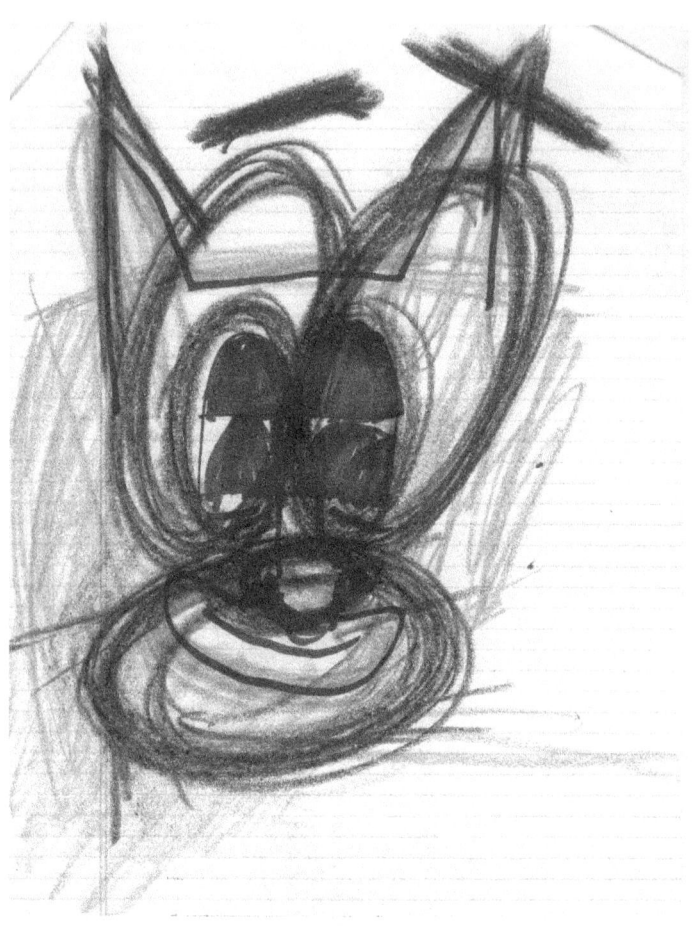

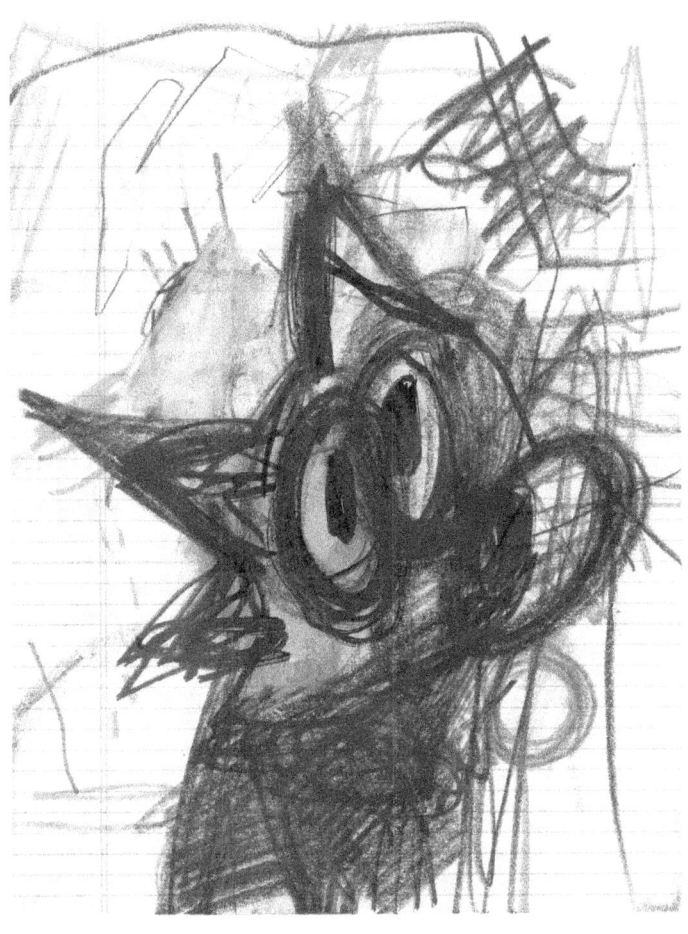

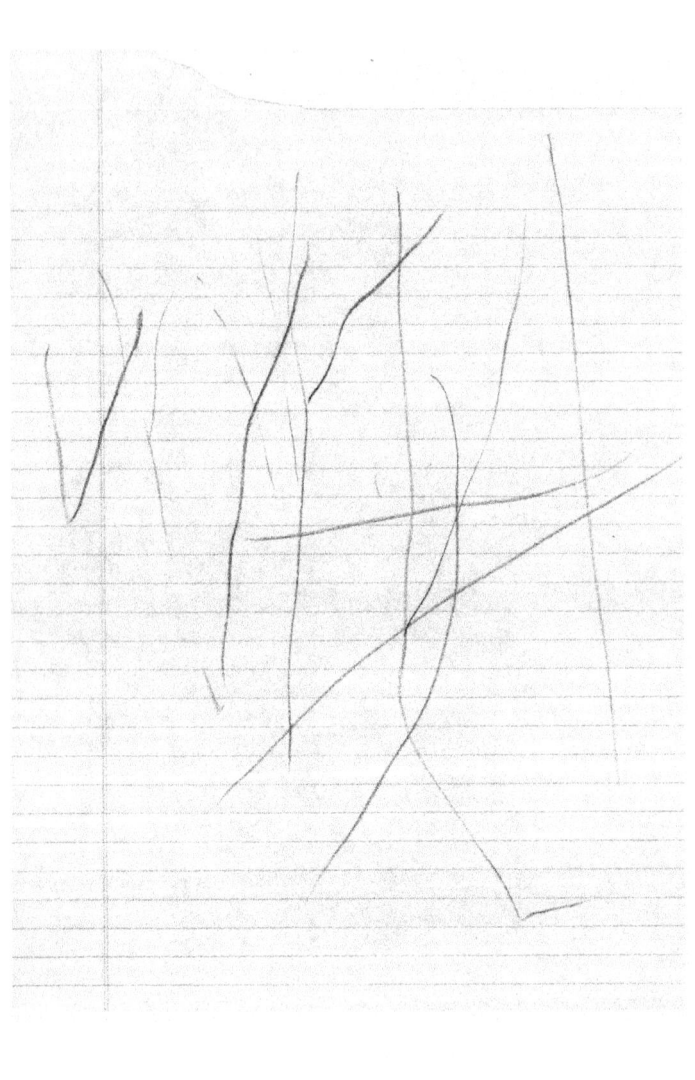

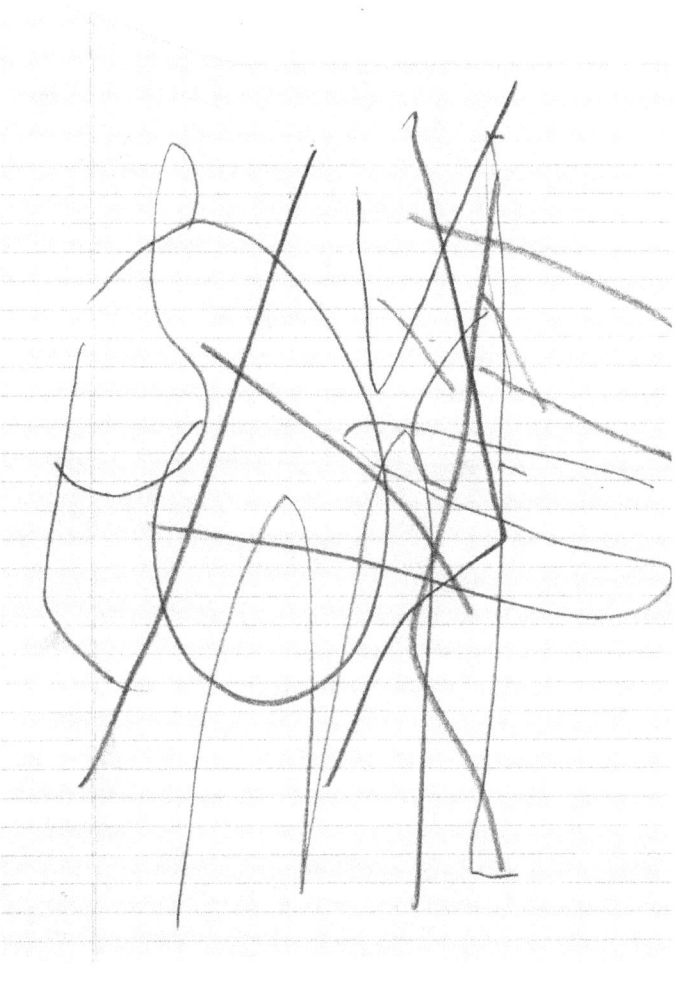

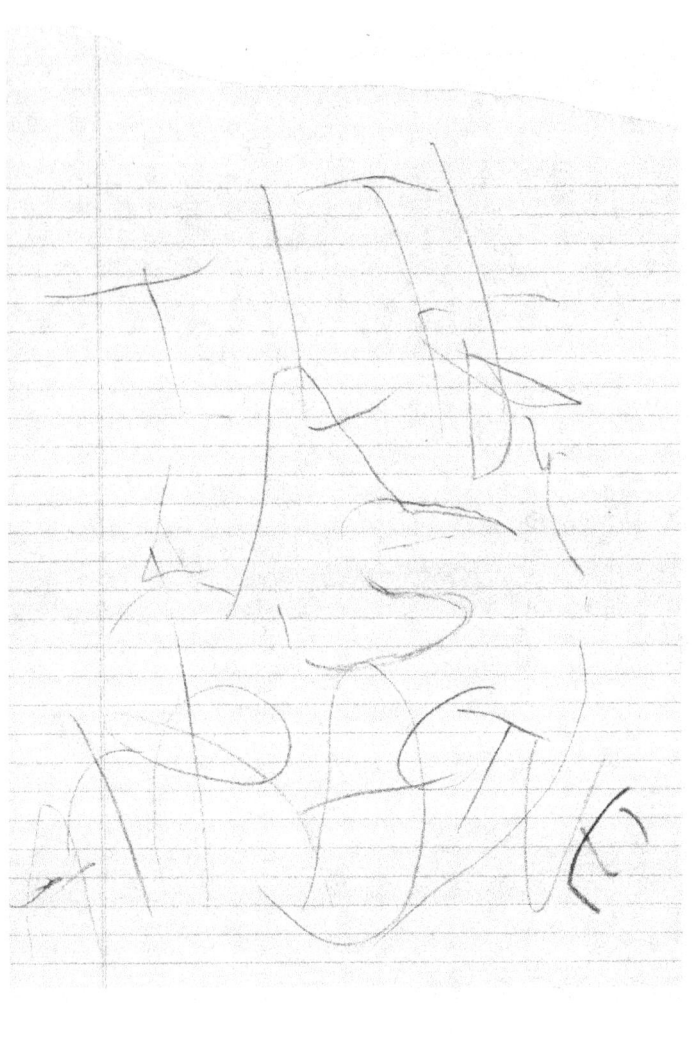

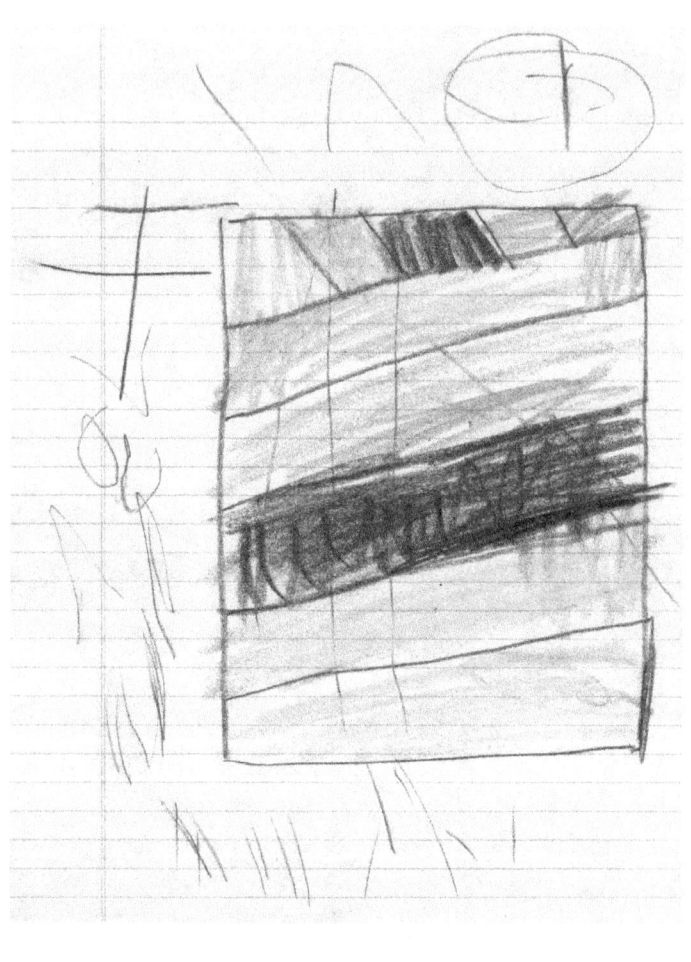

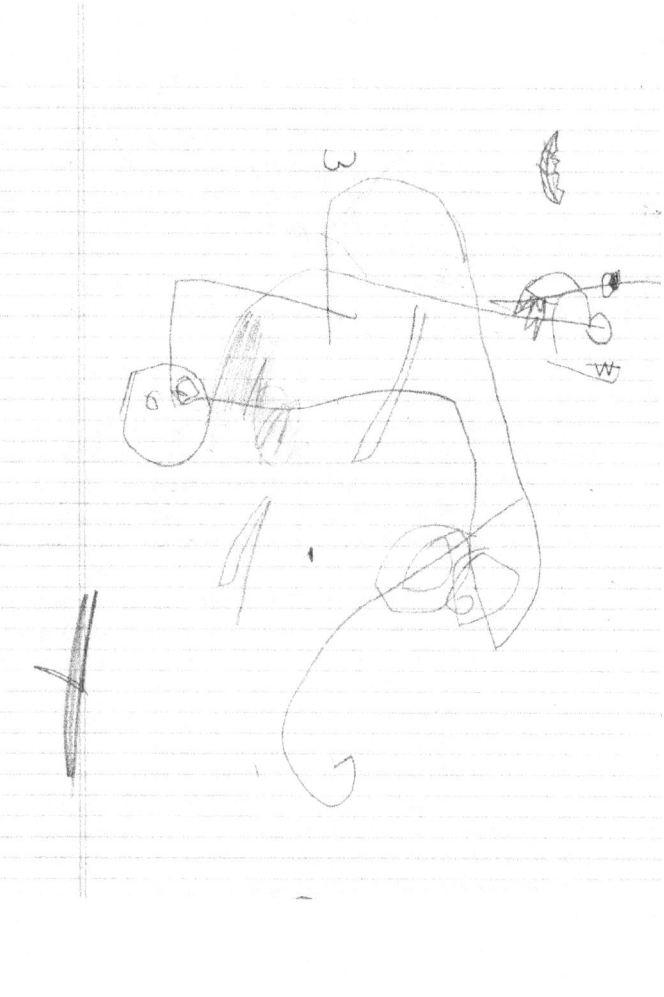

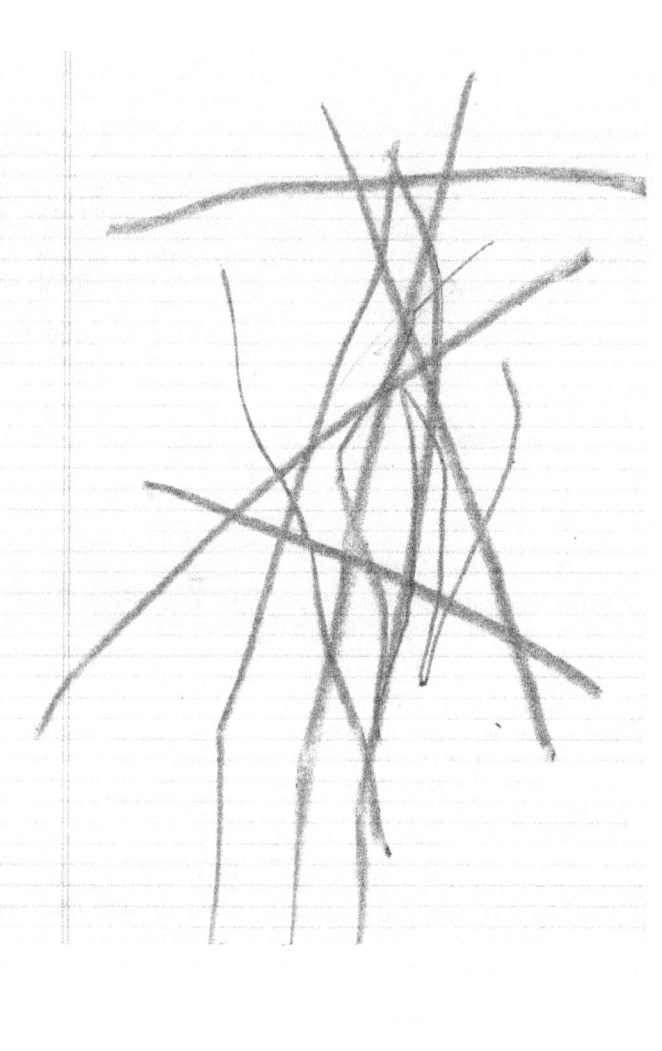

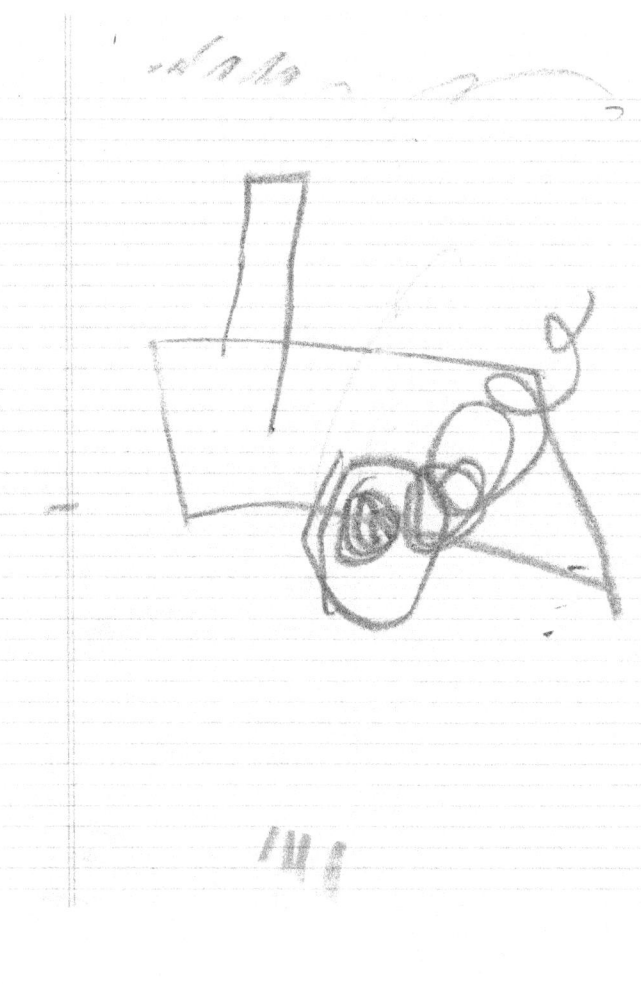

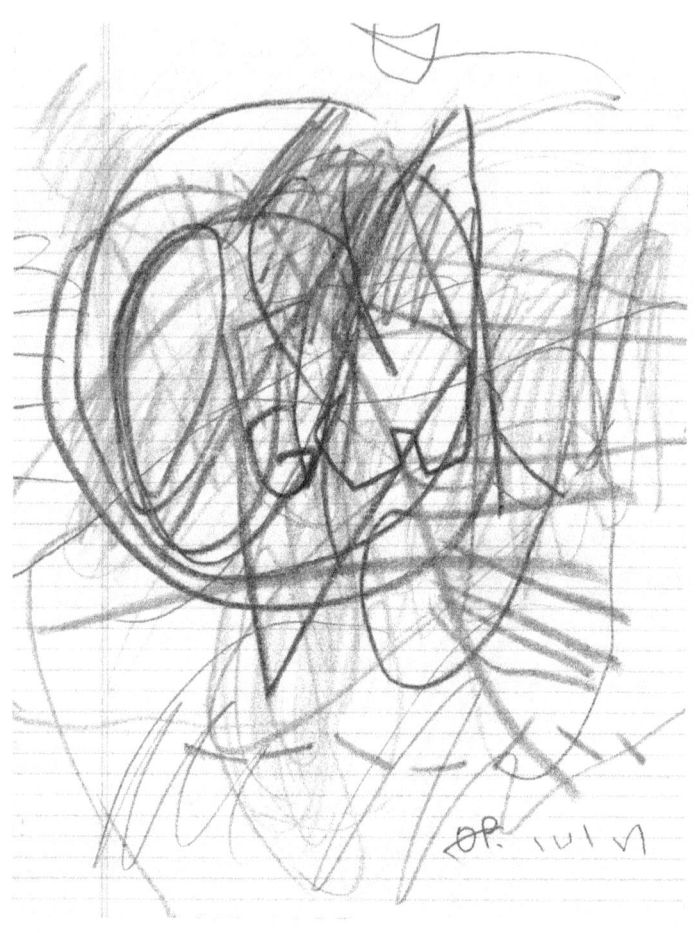

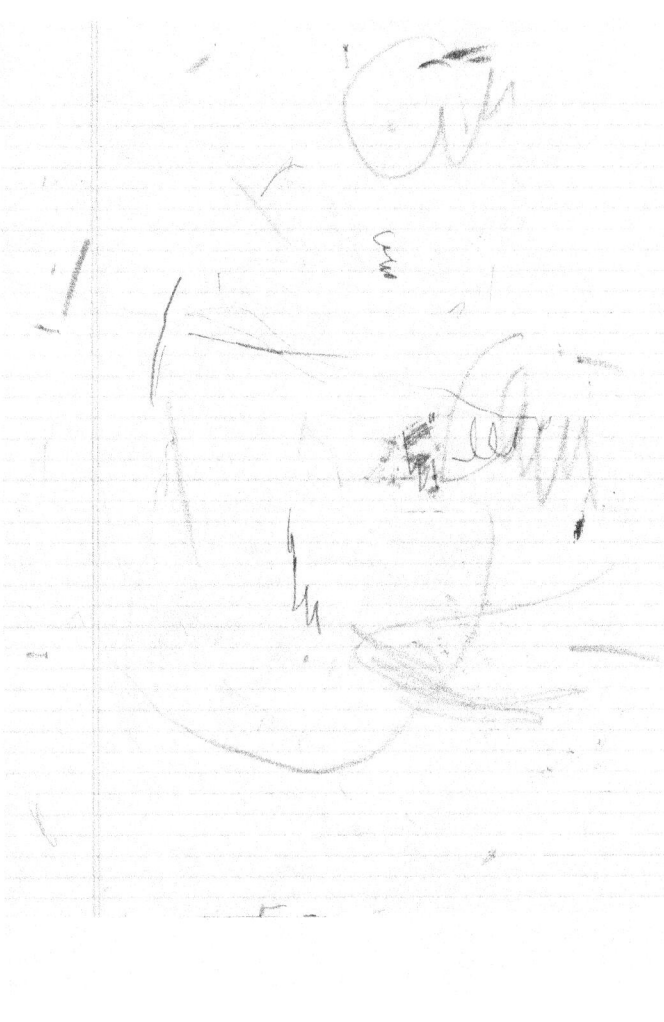

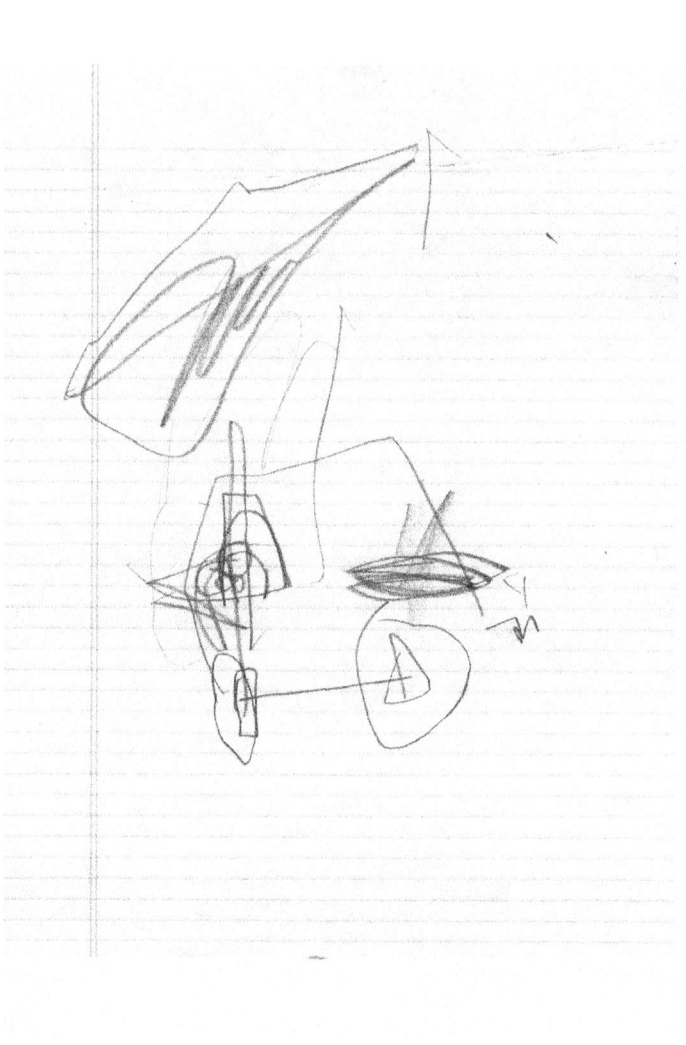

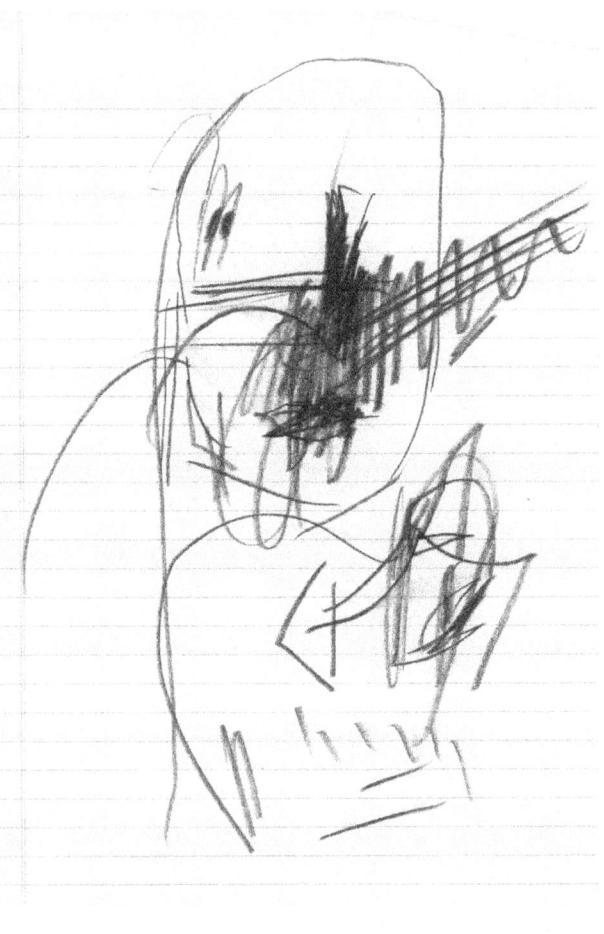

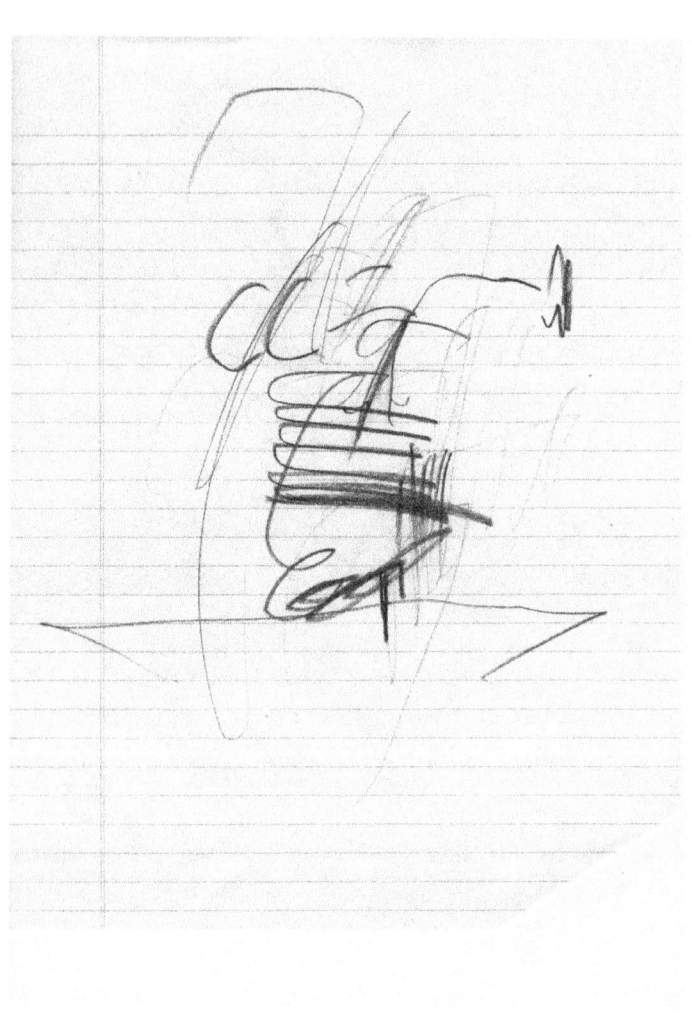

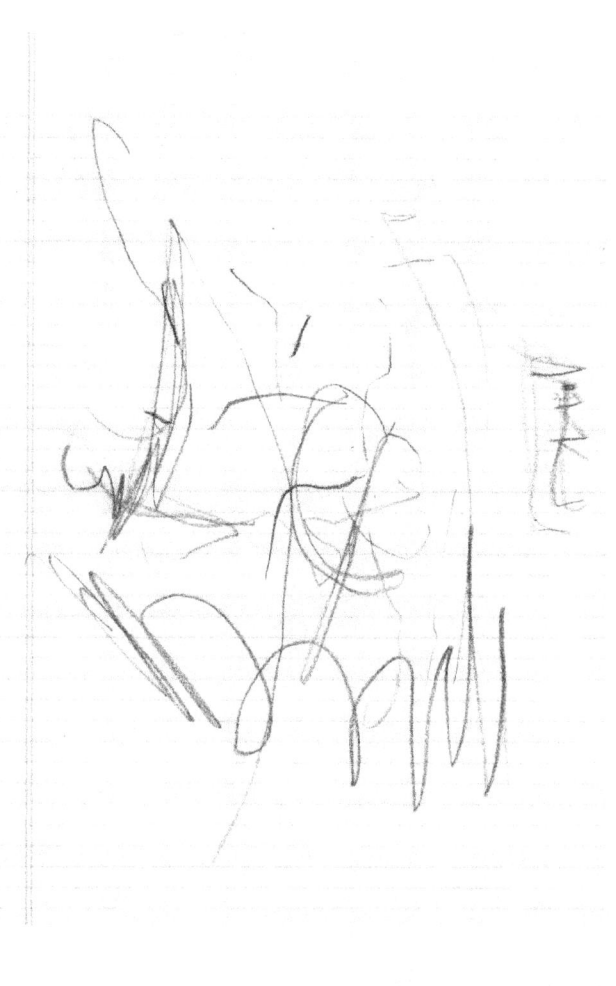

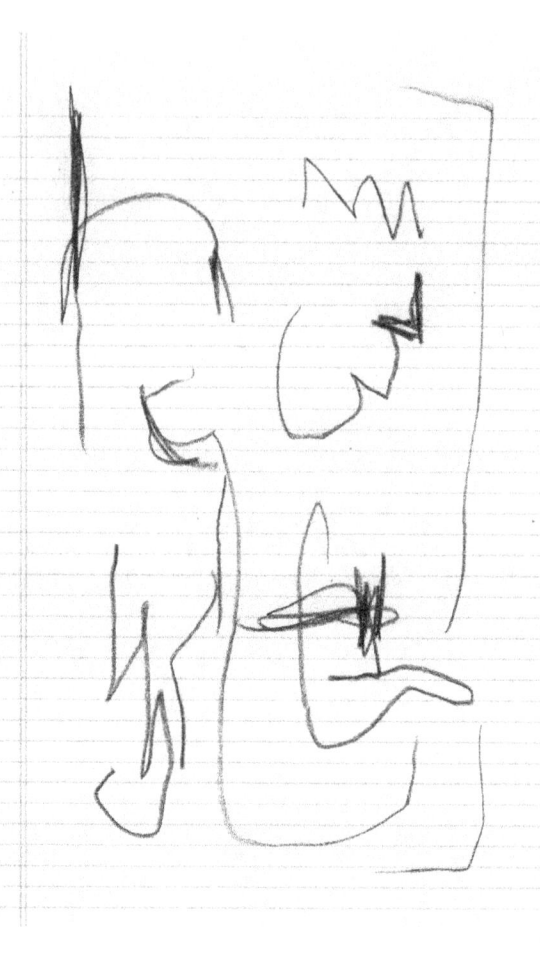

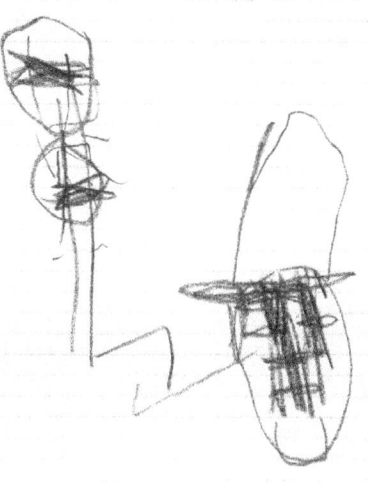

THIS

NO

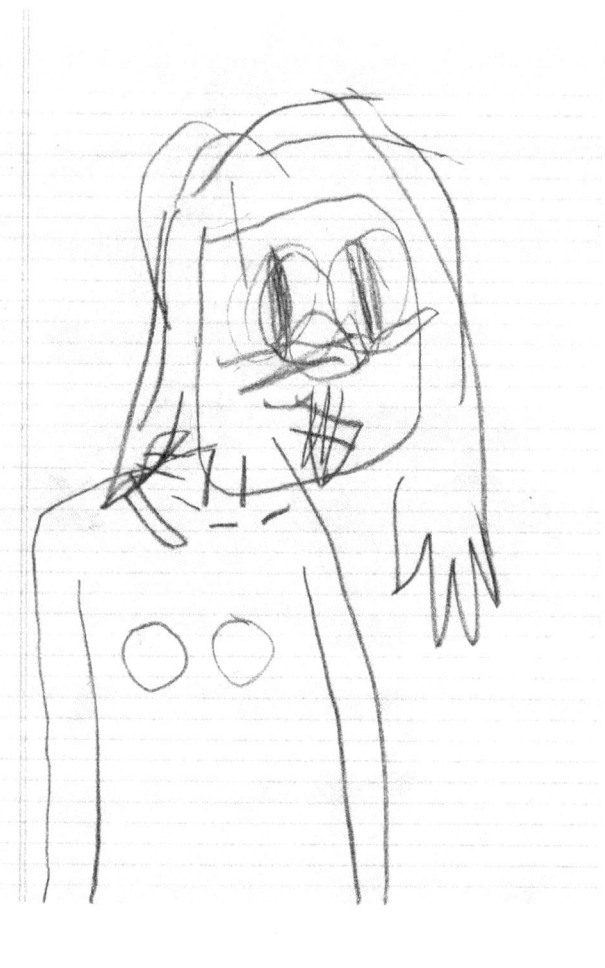

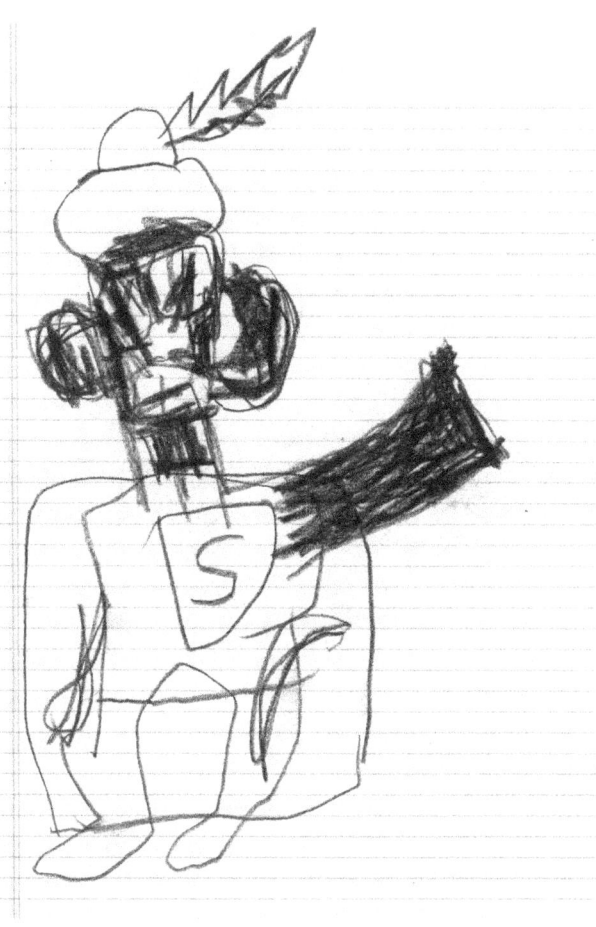

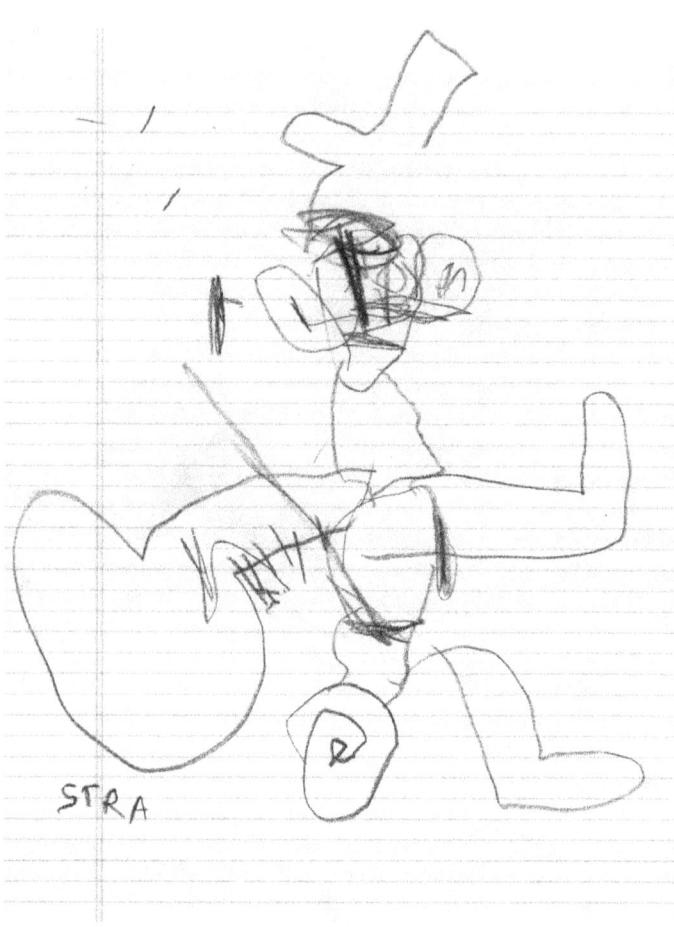

STRA

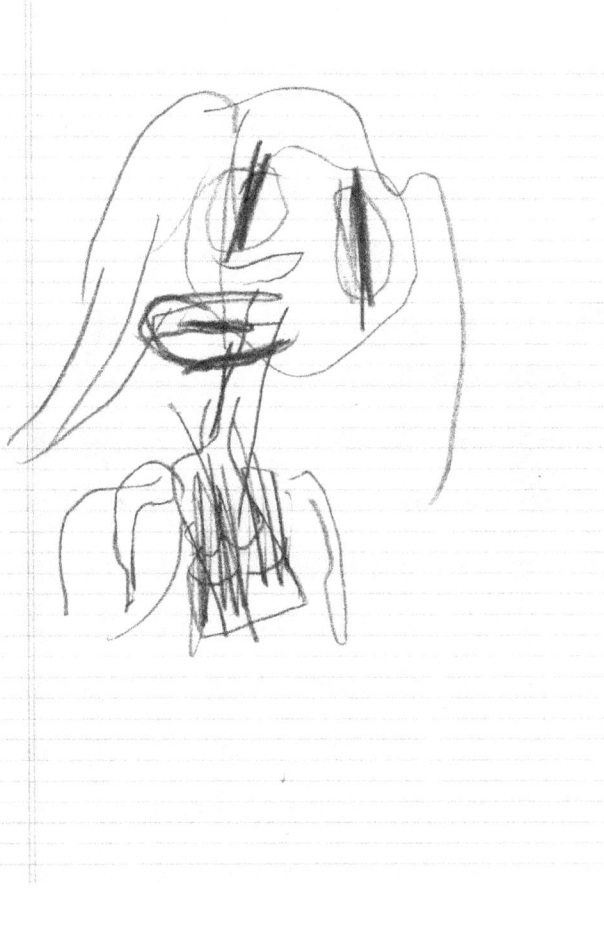

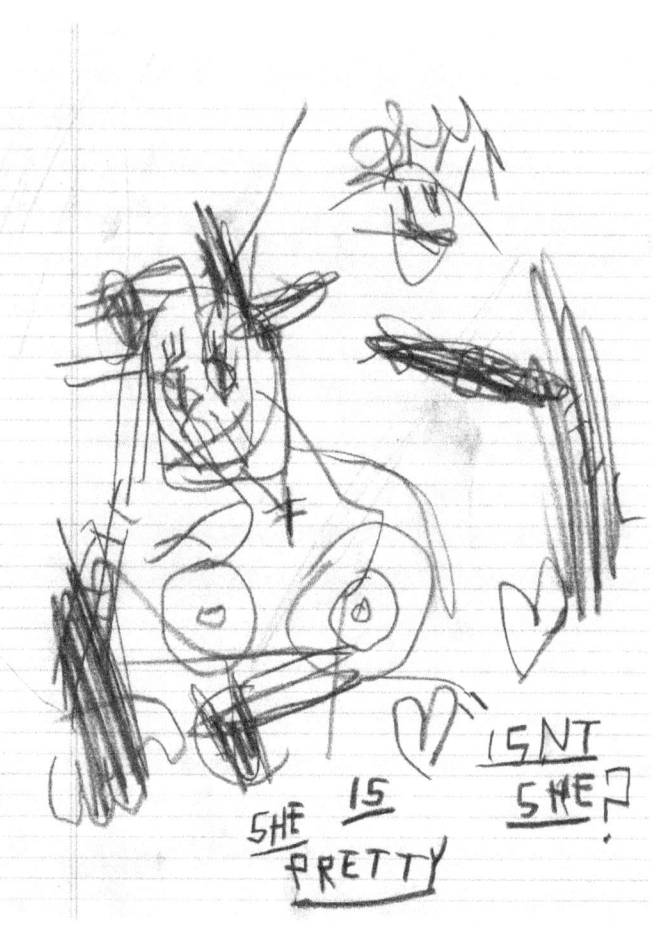

SHE IS
PRETTY

ISNT
SHE?

the
DOORS

IMAGE
OF
FEAR

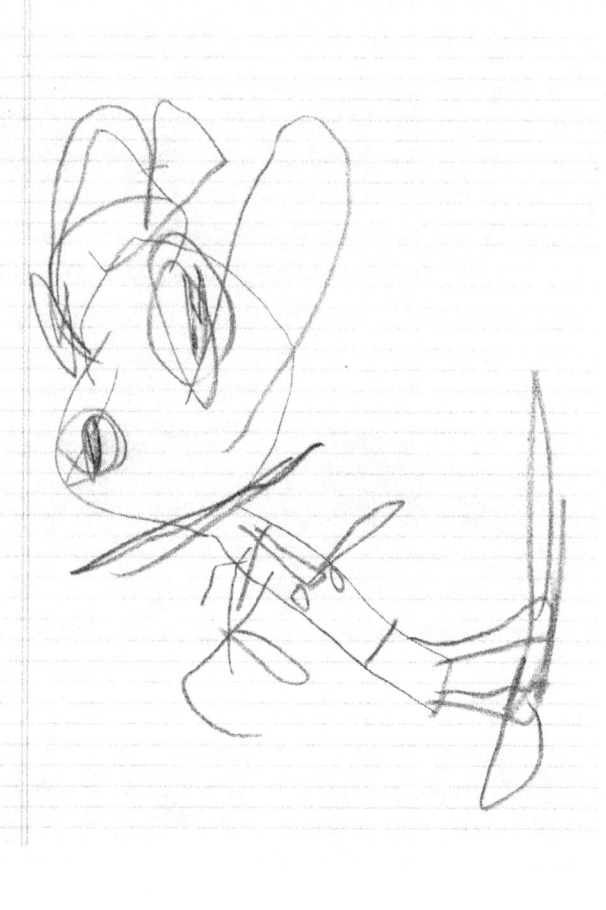

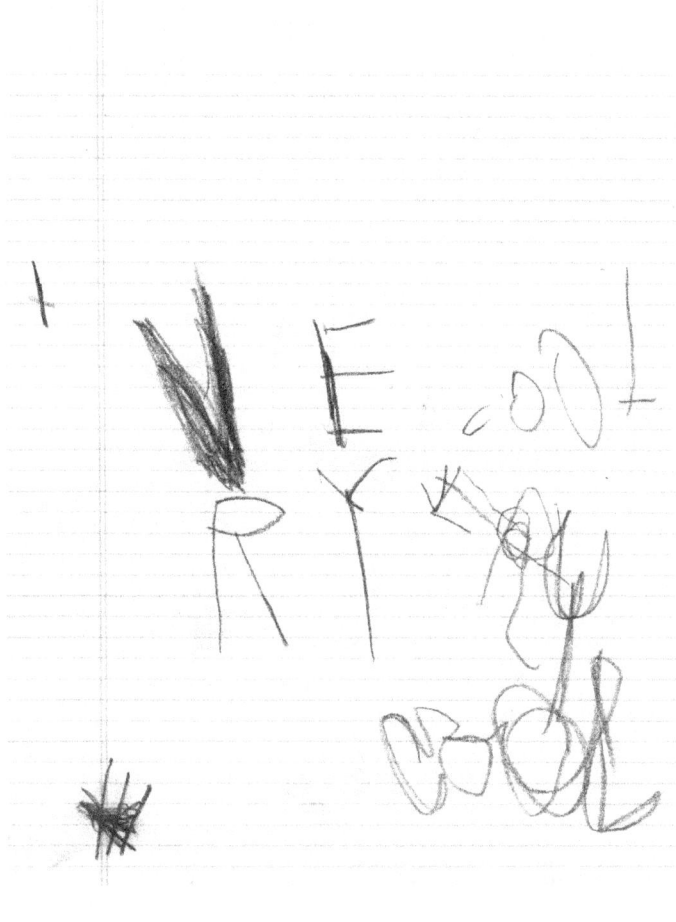

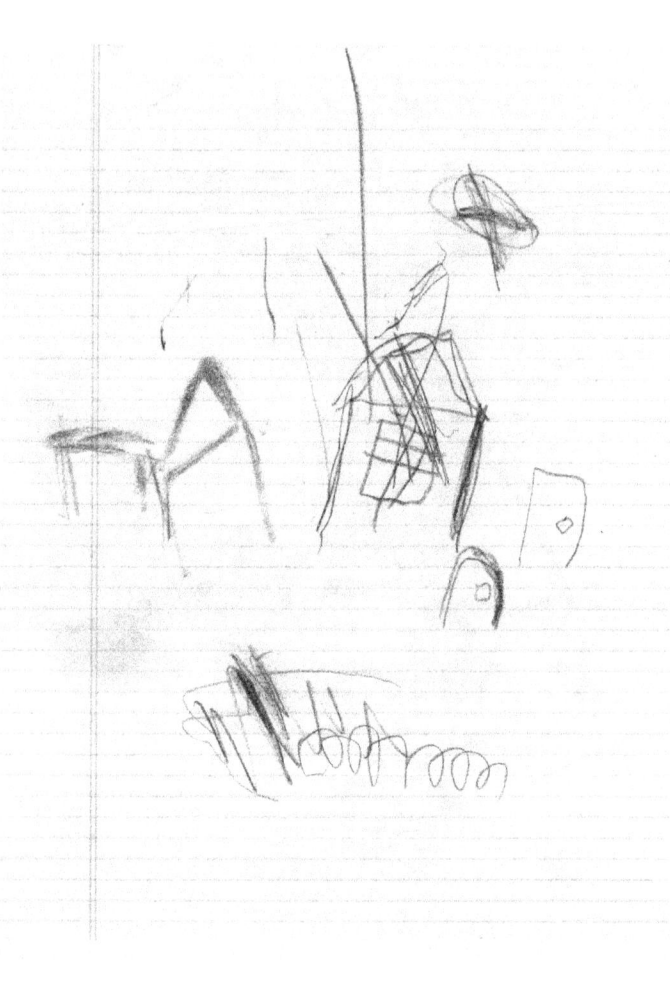

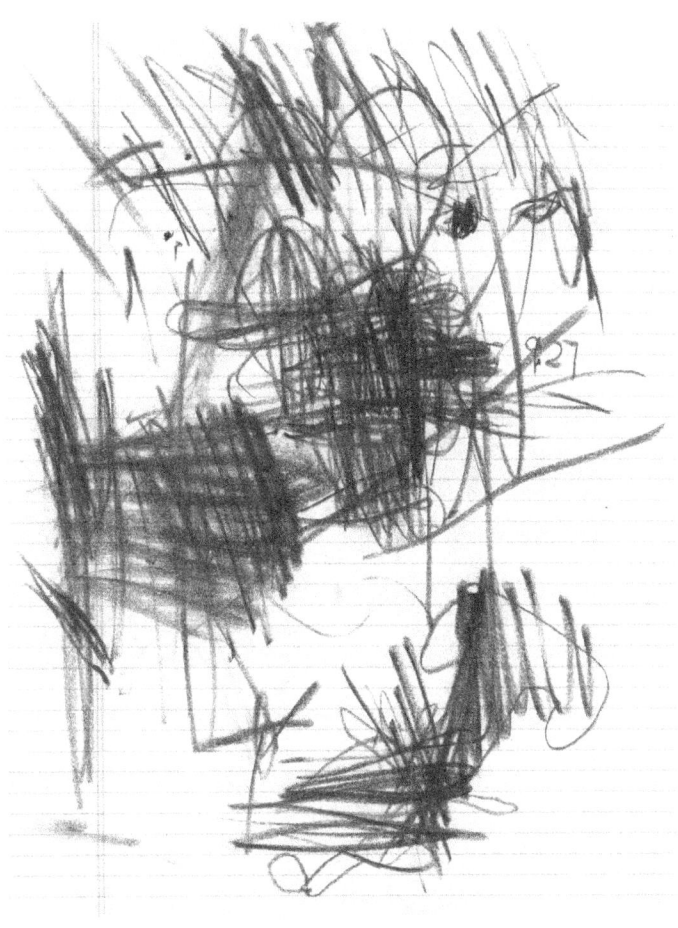

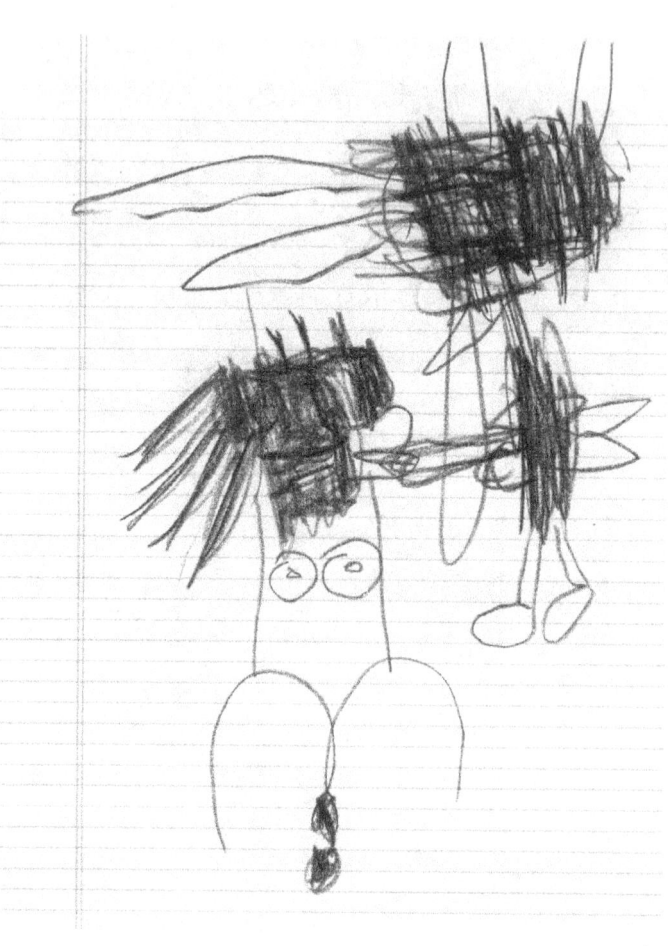

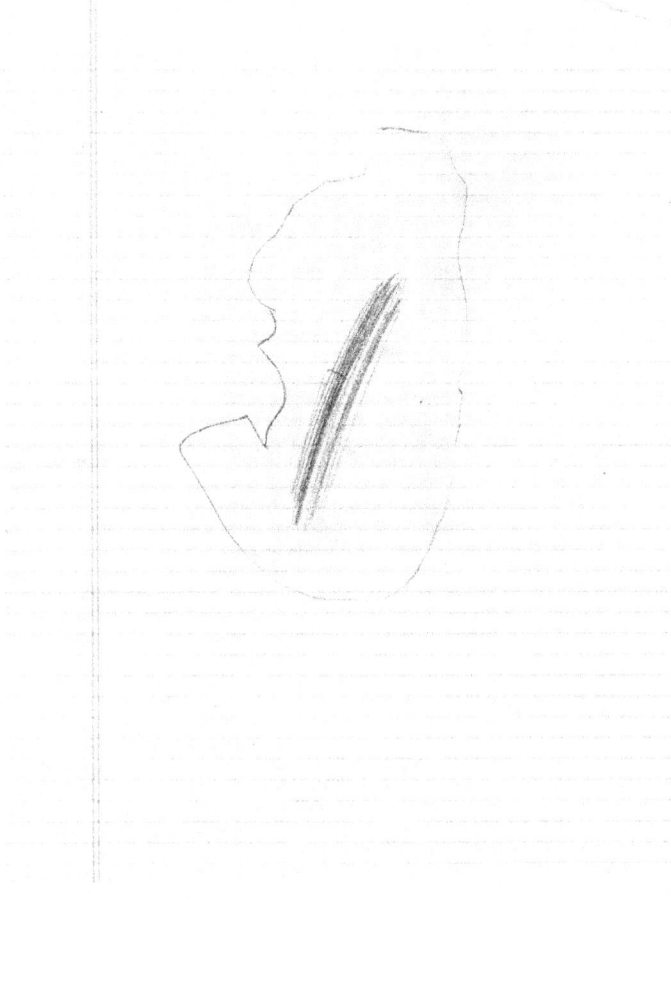

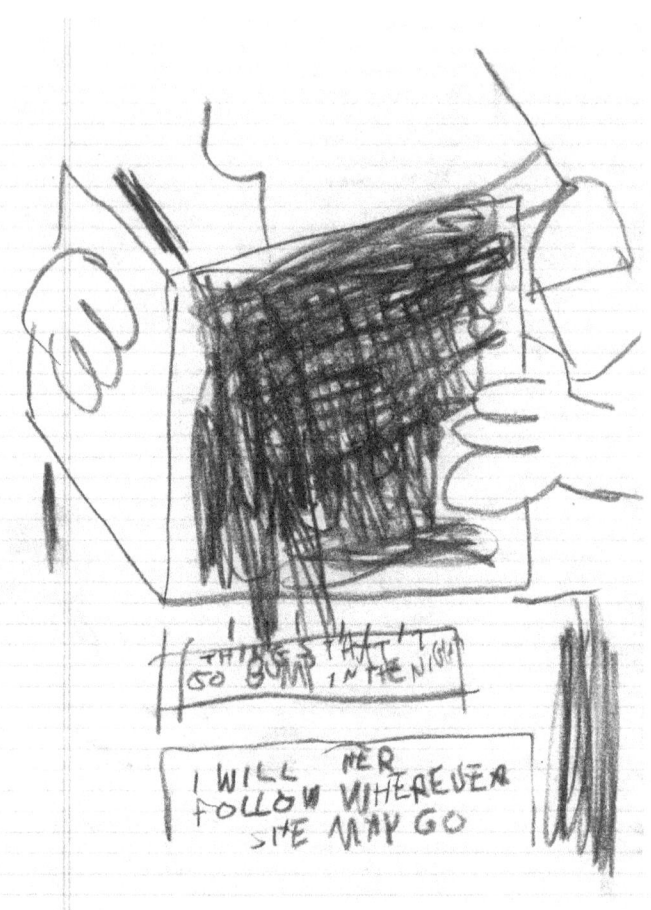

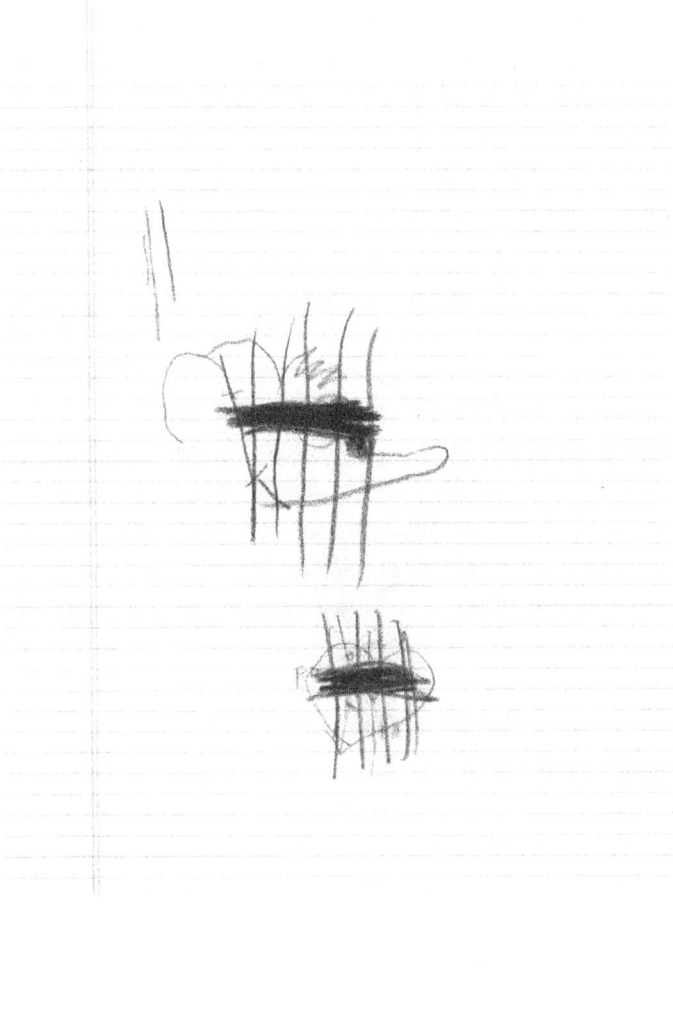

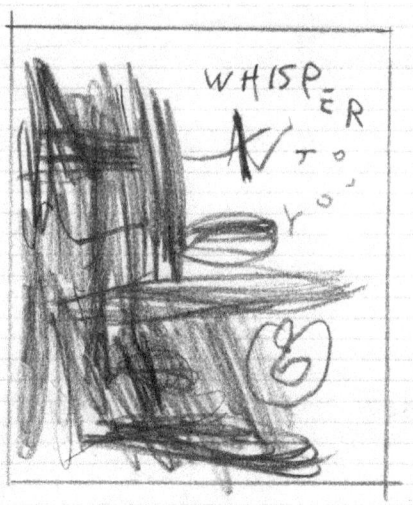

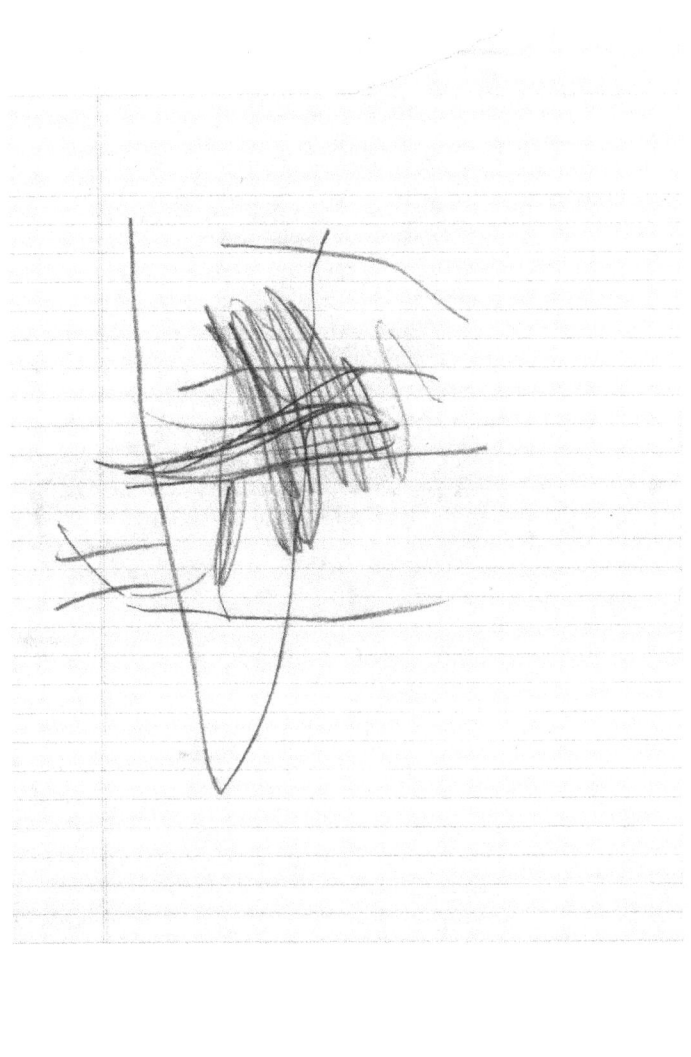

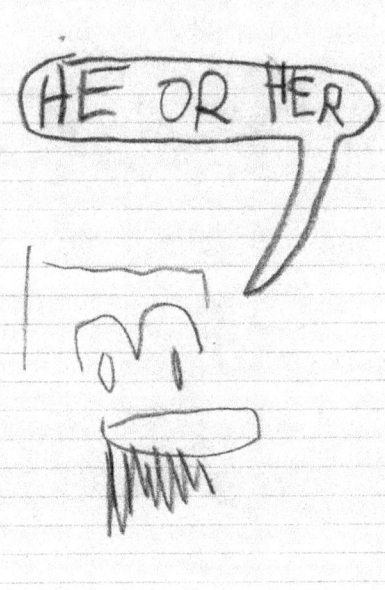

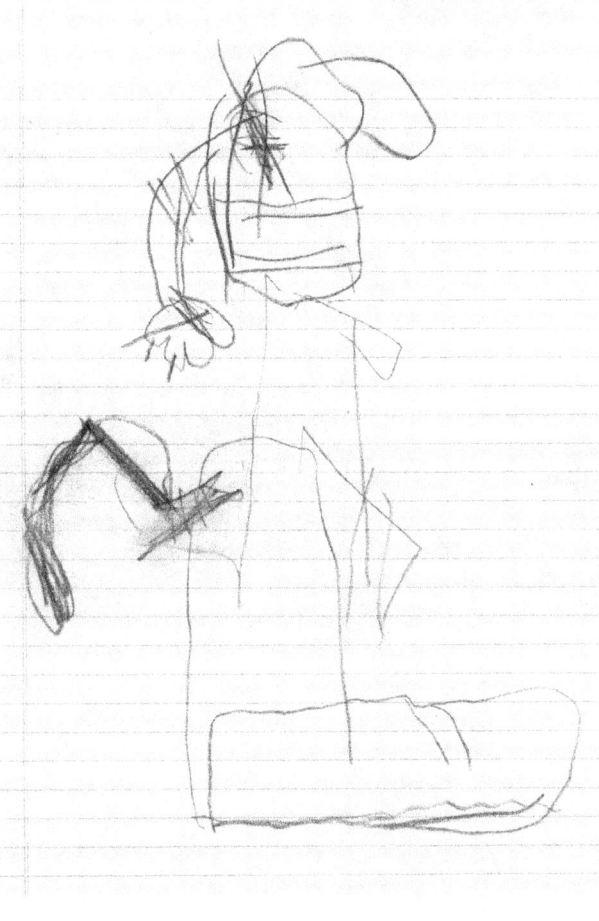

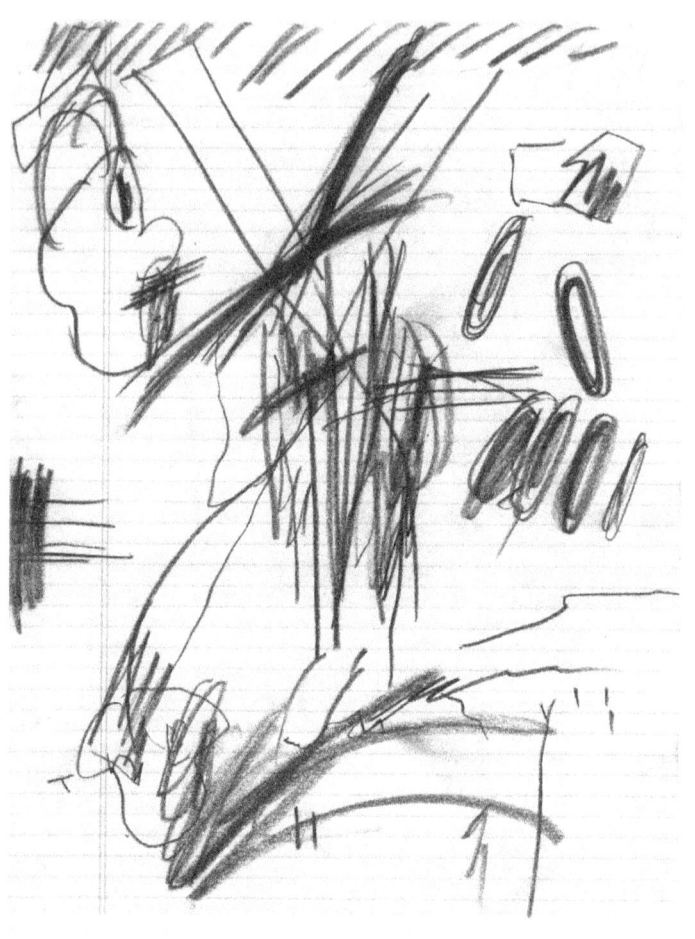

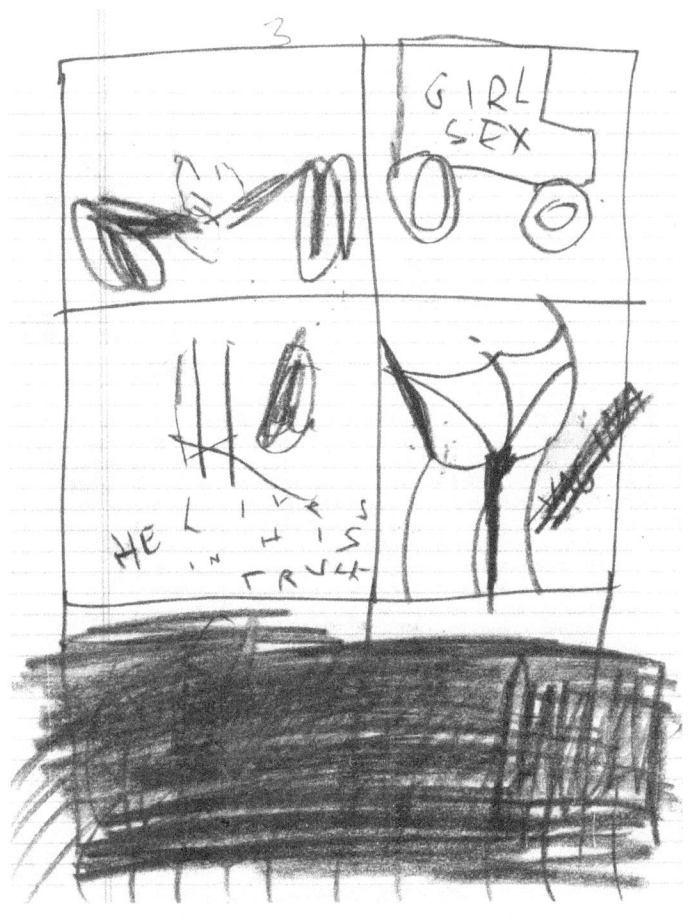

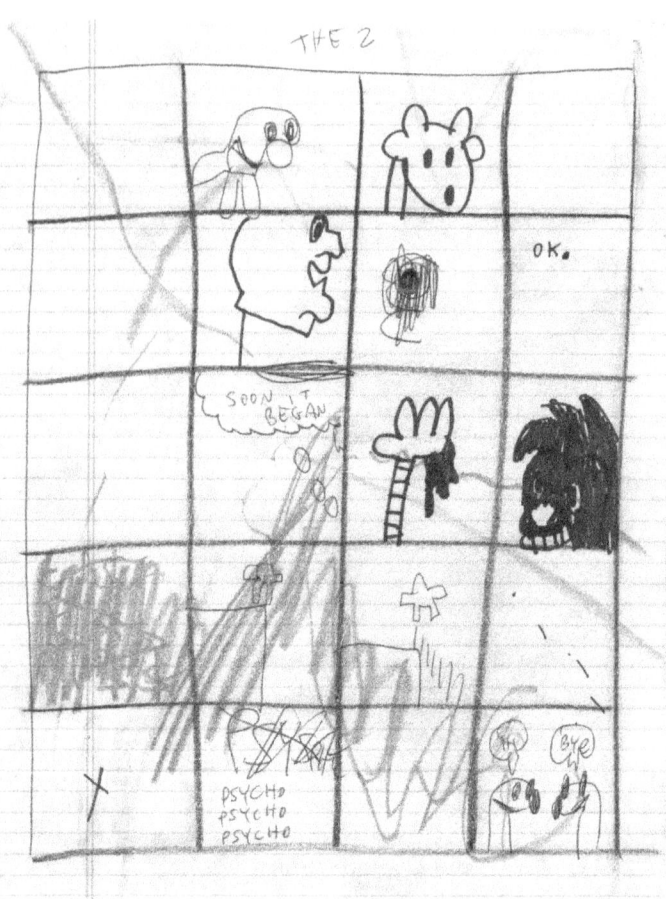

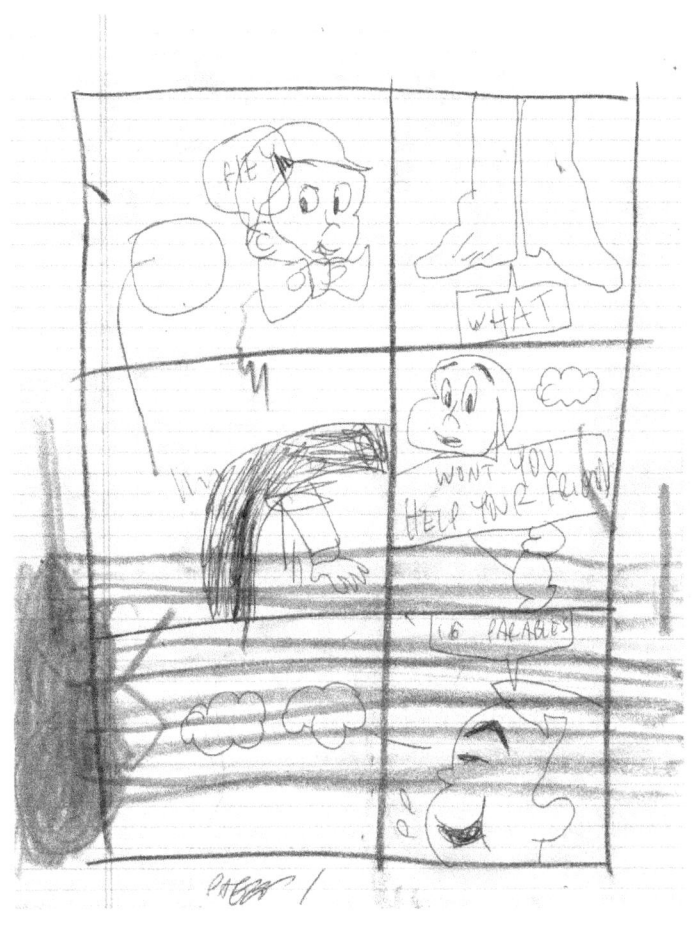

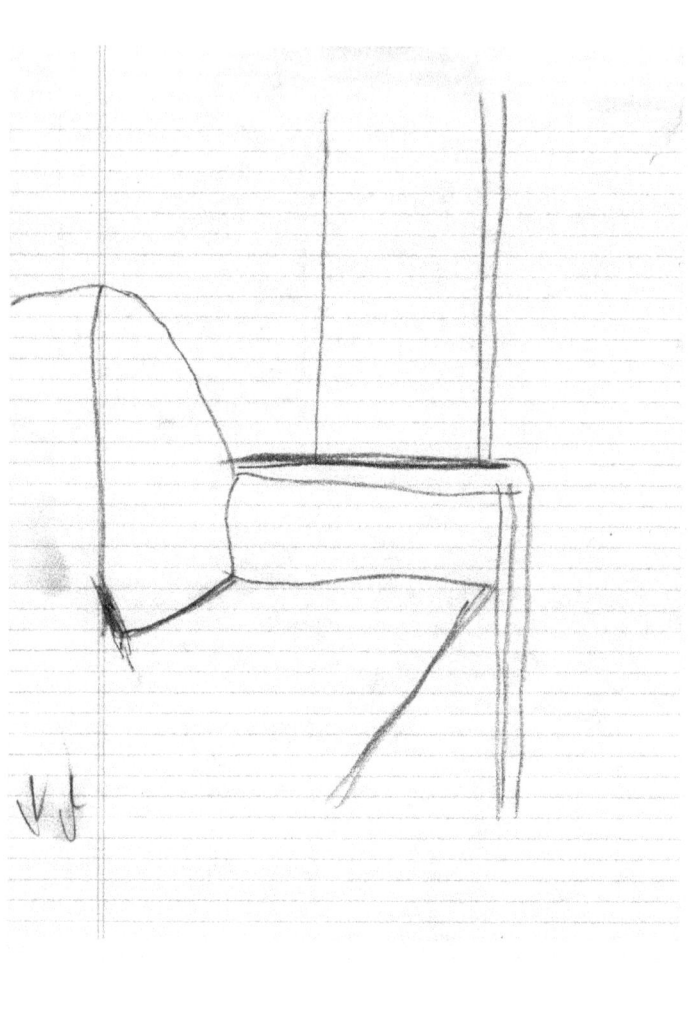

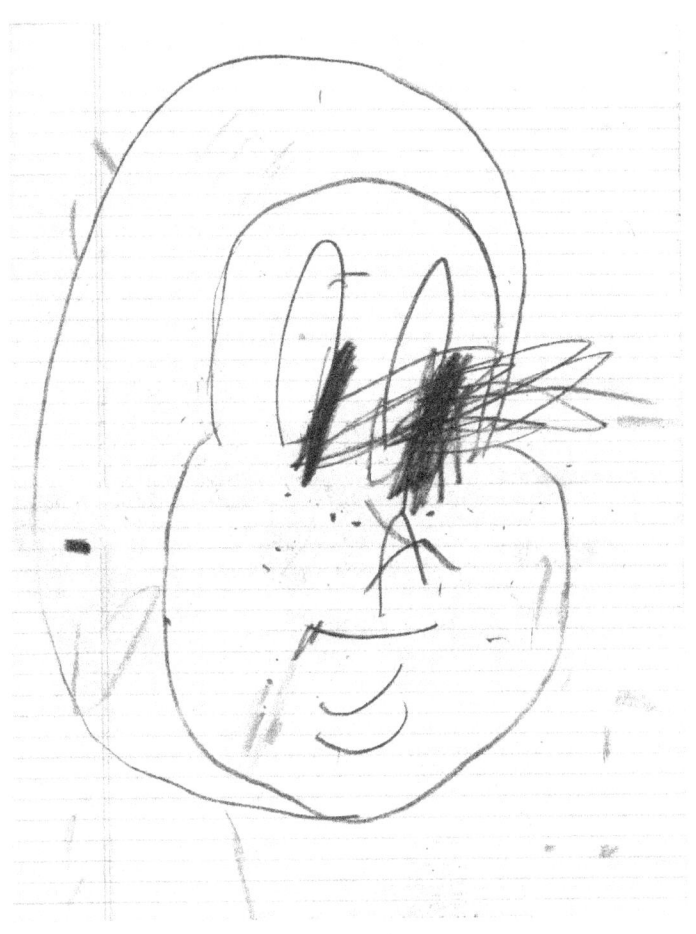

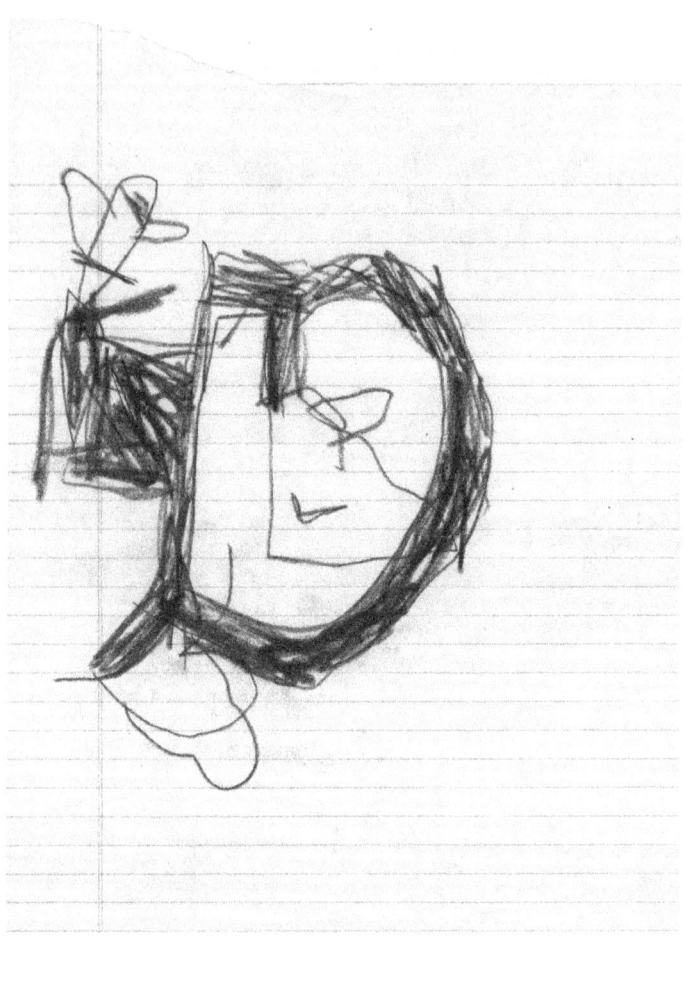

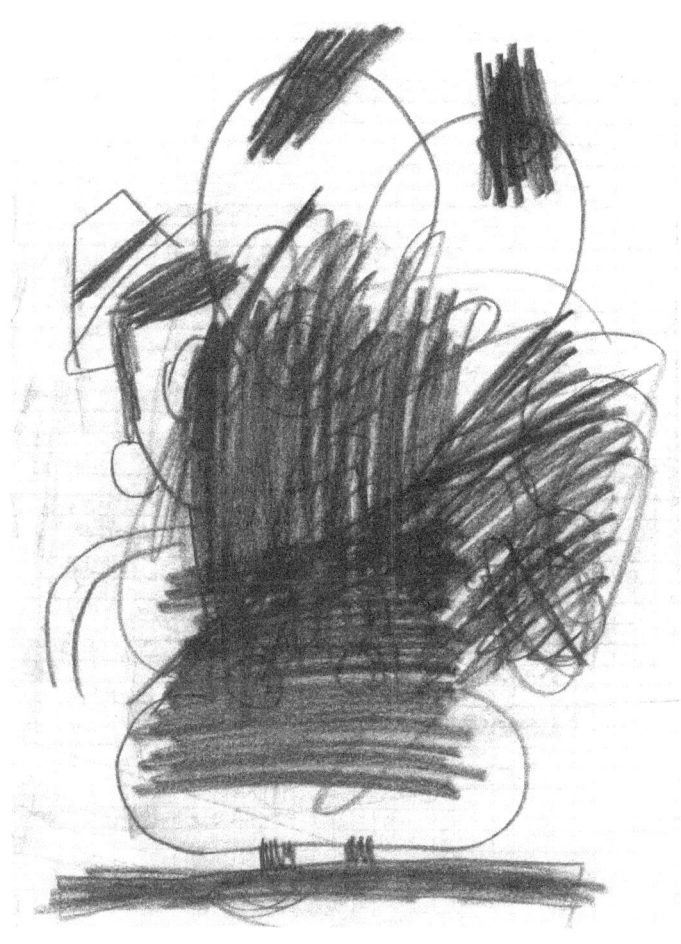

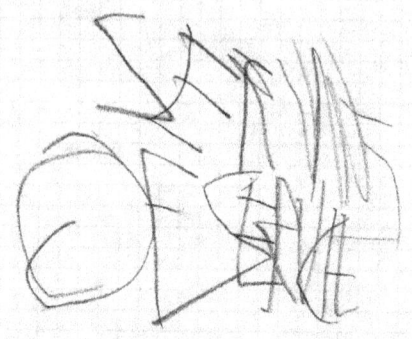

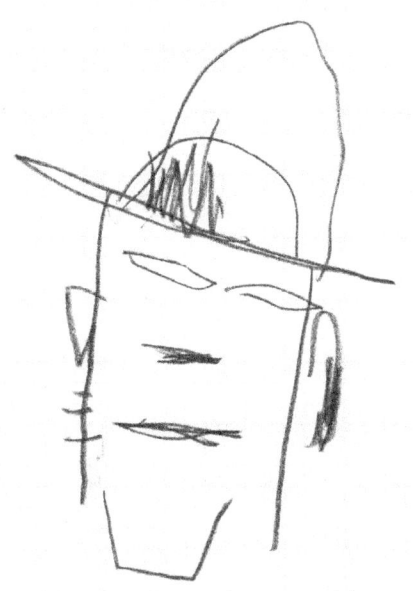

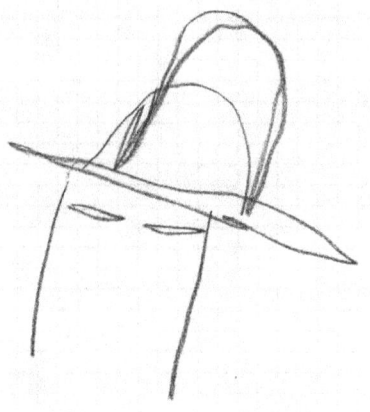

JOtn WAYNE
WAYNE

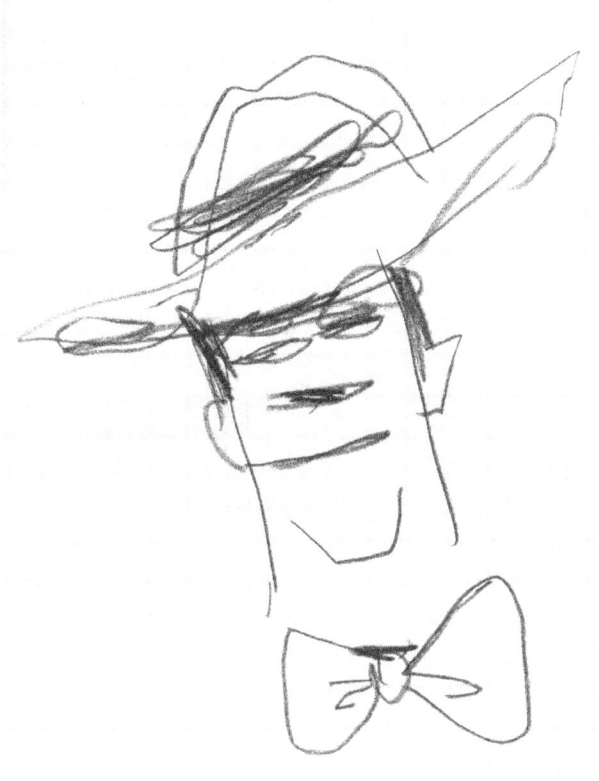

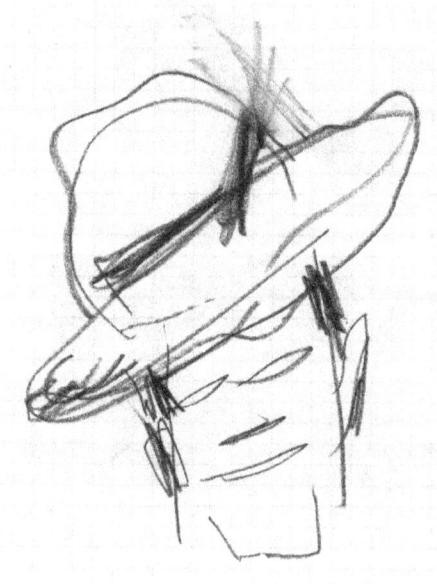

JON WAYNE

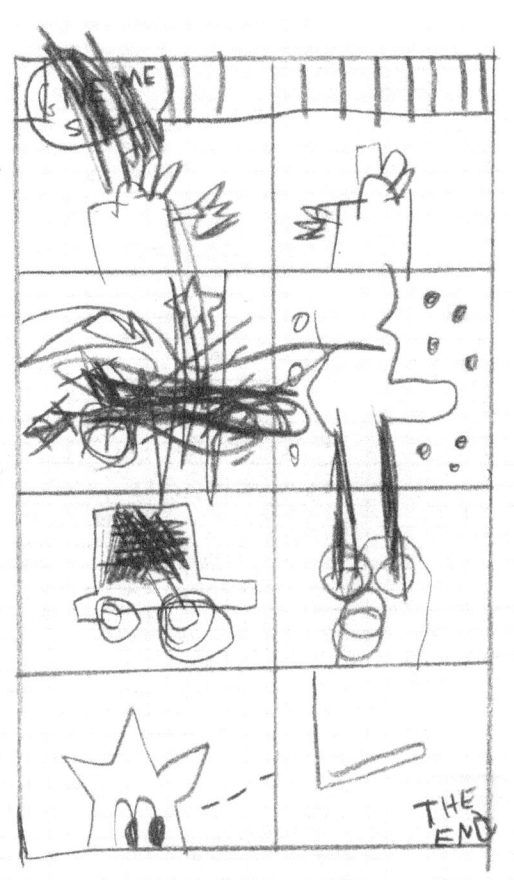

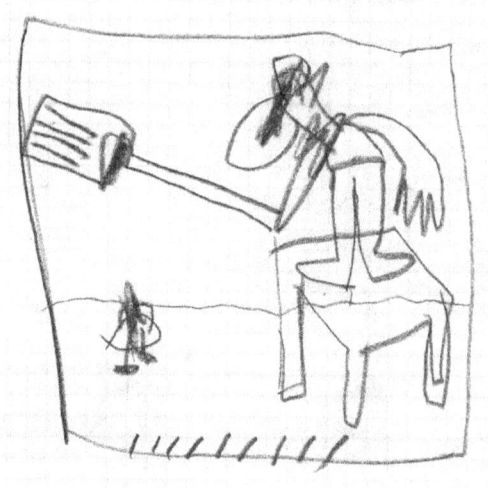

MORTIMER
MOUSE MEETS
THE MAN.

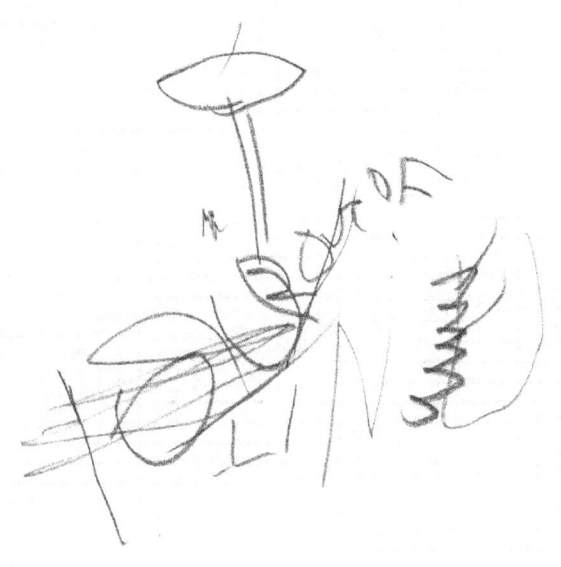

IN IT.

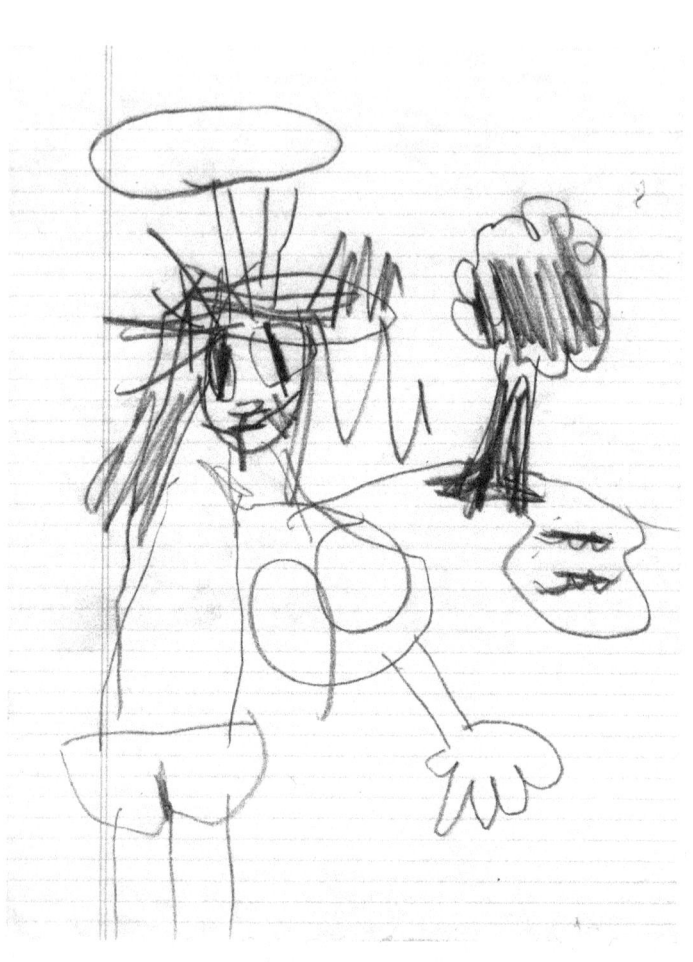

adghs ardhg[wggafhidgo ha
23t0j2[[oi [OIHTEO[H
3 2TJ320[2 2 2   2 2 2 XXXXXXXXX SHT